24clo
4/05

SUSAN SMITH

SUSAN SMITH

VICTIM OR MURDERER

GEORGE REKERS

Glenbridge Publishing Ltd.

Library of Congress Catalog Card Number: LC 95-79296

International Standard Book Number: 0-944435-38-6

Printed in the U. S. A.

Dedication

To all the children of the world who have been taken from us prematurely by their parent's own hand, and to all the missing children whose whereabouts we do not know. And to the National Center for Missing and Exploited Children, which was established by the Missing Children's Act in 1984.

Contents

List of Illustrations

Preface

Karen Tant in the Office of Marketing and Media Relations of the University of South Carolina was the first to involve me in the Susan Smith case. Fielding requests from local and national television, radio, and print journalists, she directed some initial inquiries to me. I had been willing to assist the university and the public by granting media interviews to explain how people can cope with tragic family losses.

The reports of the "kidnapping" of Michael and Alex received immediate national and international attention. I began to field the myriad of media requests for interviews and thus became familiar with the details of the tragic disappearance, and later the reported deaths of little Michael and Alex Smith.

I would like, especially, to express my appreciation for the work of the National Center for Missing and Exploited Children, and its local affiliate, the Adam Walsh Center in Columbia, South Carolina. I had been invited by President Ronald Reagan to attend a ceremony to inaugurate the National Center for Missing and Exploited Children, held in the East Room of the White House in 1984. Former United States Senator Paula Hawkins of Florida, the author of the "Missing Children's Act," the family of Adam Walsh, and the producer of the television special on Adam Walsh's tragic abduction and murder also attended that day.

The staff of the regional Adam Walsh Center in Columbia, South Carolina, assisted the Smith family after Michael and Alex were reported missing by Susan Smith.

Both the private sector and government must work hand in hand to do everything humanly possible to protect our children from those who would take and harm them.

As the publicity about the case grew, Mrs. Tant arranged for me to be interviewed by scores of TV, radio, magazine, and newspaper reporters, and she was always ready to shuttle documents, make arrangements for photographers and reporters, and to be literally "on-call" around the clock to serve the university and the public most effectively. Special thanks also to Margaret Lamb, and the staff in the USC Office of Marketing and Media Relations for all their hard work.

My oldest of five sons, Steven, brainstormed the idea of this book with me one day at home after I was asked to consider writing a book on this court case. Without the help of his creative thinking, I would not have formulated this book project. Throughout the trial, he assisted me by taking notes for me on days I could not be present. My second son, Andy, also assisted in our travel to Union, South Carolina, to work on this project. Steven took some of the photographs for the book, and never wavered in his encouragement of the project.

I also must express special appreciation to James Keene, Editor, and Mary Keene, President of Glenbridge Publishing Ltd., for their vision for this project and their unflagging efforts to get this story out to the public. Their innumerable phone calls, FAX messages, and communication smoothed the way for this publishing adventure.

I want to thank my close friend, David Lee Wilson, Jr., who is, by profession, a journalist, for his encouragement and brainstorming with me during this project. My thanks go to USC faculty colleagues, William "Bud" Gore, Ph.D., clinical psychologist, and Mark D. Kilgus, M.D., Ph.D., psychiatrist, who read major portions of this manuscript and provided constructive feedback.

And finally, my thanks to my wife, Sharon, and my five terrific sons, Steven, Andy, Matt, Tim, and Mark, for their understanding and patience while I often "burned the midnight oil" completing this manuscript.

Introduction

The high ceiling and hardwood furnishings of the eighty-two-year-old Union County Courtroom give the chamber very poor acoustics, so it was difficult to understand everything that Susan Smith's soft-spoken defense attorney, David Bruck, said when he strayed from the microphone. But now, Mr. Bruck listens intently, with one finger pressed to his forehead as his witness, Dr. Seymour Hallek, speaks clearly into the microphone on the witness stand. Professor Hallek had been hired by the defense to conduct a psychiatric evaluation of Susan Smith, and he was describing what Susan told him:

"As she is driving, she is constantly crying. Uncharacteristically for her, she turns off the car radio. She finds her body shaking uncontrollably. She feels nauseous. During that one-hour drive, she bit her nails off completely.

"She's driving, thinking that she has to kill herself because there is nobody around who cares for her. She feels she's lost everybody.

". . . she almost ran off the road because she's shaking and so distressed.

1

"The main thought she had was that she had to die. Before she got [to the John D. Long Lake], she felt that she had to take the kids with her . . . because she was concerned they would live without a mother.

"All this is irrational. She was not thinking rationally at that point. With her strong religious convictions, she firmly believed that the children would go to heaven."

Straying again from the microphone, her attorney, David Bruck, leans forward slightly and dramatically asks, "Why didn't Susan go into the water?"

"I can only reach the assumption that when she ran out of the car, that her self-preservation instincts took over, and although up to that moment she fully intended to kill herself, she got frightened," Dr. Halleck replied.

This was part of one person's interpretations of the events leading to the tragic deaths of three-year-old Michael Daniel Smith and his fourteen-month-old brother, Alexander Tyler Smith. And yet, Dr. Halleck referred to a "defect" (his term) in the manner in which he came to his view, because he had not visited the lake where the drownings occurred to compare Susan's descriptions to him with the physical geography of that spot. The attorneys also questioned him and found that he was uninformed about other crucial details in Susan Smith's life.

But did Professor Halleck's description fit Susan, nevertheless? For the vast majority of the American public who were shut out from firsthand observation of the proceedings because of the judge's camera ban, there are bits and pieces of testimony and evidence like this that need to be put together like a giant puzzle to get the whole picture.

Months before the trial, Circuit Court Judge William Howard ordered a mental evaluation of Susan Vaughan

Smith because her defense attorney indicated he would enter either a plea of "not guilty by reason of insanity" or a plea of "guilty but mentally ill." My colleague at the University of South Carolina (USC) School of Medicine, Professor Donald Morgan, M.D., Sc.D.,[1] was the lead doctor conducting the state mental evaluation through the affiliated teaching hospital, the William S. Hall Psychiatric Institute. But state law and Judge Howard's "gag" order prohibited Dr. Morgan from speaking to the press before and during the trial.

The University of South Carolina media office agreed with the hospital director, Larry Faulkner, M.D., that calls from the press be forwarded to the USC media office and that I would be the spokesperson to the press, answering their questions about the procedures for a mental evaluation, about the meaning of psychological terms used in the court proceedings, and concerning any other questions posed by TV, radio and print media journalists. I could ethically and legally serve as a USC hospital spokesperson because I had never been involved in directly examining Susan Smith as a patient.[2]

As information became available in the pre-trial months and during the Susan Smith trial, I was available to the press on countless occasions to help them assist the public to better understand the clinical information coming out on the puzzling mind of a mother in this tragic case of the death of the two beautiful little boys, Michael and Alex.

Unprecedented heavy media attention has been given to this particular case of parental child murder, even though there have reportedly been between 1600 to 2000 such cases annually over the past decade. There has been considerable speculation as to why the public is so interested in this story. But one thing is clear: The true story of Susan Smith and her family contains all the profound dramatic themes regarding human vice and virtue of our civilization's greatest literature:

- Death versus life
- Deception versus truth
- Betrayal versus loyalty
- Abuse versus protection
- Excuse versus responsibility
- Cruelty versus love
- Sorrow versus remorse, and
- Guilt versus forgiveness

While I related various aspects of the Susan Smith case to the reporters regarding psychological theory and research, the investigative reporters also provided me with extensive inside information on the case as it developed before and during the trial. I compared this information to what I learned from attending the trial myself and from my own interviews of individuals in Union, South Carolina. When possible, I have attempted to verify the facts of this story as they came out over many months in the press. I have read countless newspaper and magazine articles, listened to numerous radio broadcasts, and viewed television news broadcasts. I have also read Gary Henderson's book on the search for the reported missing Smith boys, *Nine Days in Union*, and Maria Eftimiades's book on Susan Smith's hoax and confession prior to the trial, *Sins of the Mother*, and David Smith's book *Beyond All Reason*.

If Susan Smith were my patient, I would have been legally prohibited from writing about her case because of confidentiality laws. This book is based upon the publicly available facts, primarily from the Susan Smith trial itself, which consisted of public sworn testimony, and by interviews with individuals whose comments are public knowledge.

The key question I have addressed is the question, Why? Why did Susan V. Smith do what she did? Various views were expressed during the trial. The jury found Susan guilty of two counts of murder, finding her guilty of harboring malice against her two little boys.

On the other hand, mental health experts, social workers, and school counselors testified as to Susan's history of depression, suicidal thoughts and actions, and adjustment problems in the context of her tragic loss of her father to suicide, her sexual abuse by her stepfather, and her growing up in a dysfunctional family with a family tree replete with multiple cases of depression and alcoholism.

Psychological and psychiatric experts also testified as to Susan's mental state before and during the commission of her crime. Susan's defense lawyers painted a picture of an intermittently depressed young woman who "snapped." She planned her suicide together with killing her children to "take them with her," but then "botched" her suicide by killing her boys but not herself. Is Susan a victim herself, not a true murderer?

Bits and pieces of the story told in court have been broadcast to the nation and to the world. But "sound bites" do not contain sufficient information to understand this unusually complex case. But our mind keeps asking, Why? "Why did she kill her own helpless little children?"

Psychology can help us understand what was going on at the time of the crime. Psychology can help us understand the impact of Susan's experiences, the suicide of her father, and the sexual abuse by her stepfather. Psychology can also help us examine the "abuse excuse" and assist us in putting the pieces of this frustrating puzzle together. Perhaps we can then begin to make some sense of a crime that will not be forgotten.

Competing theories of what was going on in Susan's mind have been offered in court and out of court. Within the limitations of the data available to me, I have presented the Susan Smith story with the help of psychological explanation, psychological research, and psychological theory. This is not the final word. Others have offered some plausible explanations, which may be legitimate and contain some truth. But my effort to understand the Susan Smith story as a member of the public and as a psychologist, will hopefully get us closer to understanding the sad and tragic truth about the life of Susan Smith and the deaths of her two dear little boys.

1

The Unthinkable Crime
Why Did Susan Kill Her Own Babies?

Rushing through the automated glass doors of the entrance, Susan looked up and focused on the high ceiling with its bright fluorescent lights at the Winn-Dixie supermarket where she was reporting for work. "What an open, inviting environment," she thought, "I wonder why I never noticed that it's the bright lighting that makes this place so cheery for me."

She approached the time clock in the employee workroom with a sense of rising anticipation. She became aware that her heart was beginning to pound. Why?

It was just another workday, but Susan felt that she had every reason to expect the best today. Yes, it seemed almost certain that David was not only noticing her lately, but she suspected—or shall we say "hoped"—that his glances meant something even more. And the more she daydreamed, the more she wondered if her dreams were coming true. She was extremely curious this morning to find out if her hopes would be realized.

"Maybe it was the way he smiled at me yesterday that gave me the impression that he is definitely interested in me," she wondered as she stood at the time clock, absorbed in thought. A warm, pleasant feeling accompanied even the thought of David, and she could hardly wait for her workday to begin.

"David *is* a little bit on the quiet and shy side," she mused about her favorite co-worker at Winn-Dixie, "but he's so *handsome* and *so* very eligible. I wonder . . . does he really like me? Does he think I'm special?"

Susan hadn't even finished clocking in when she heard his gentle voice behind her, "Good morning, Susan." In an instant, that little element of uncertainty melted away when David put his hand on Susan's left arm.

With a longing gaze into her eyes, David gently asked, "How are you doin' today?"

Her emotions soared.

"Just fine. Especially when I can look forward to working here with you, David," she replied with a wink. She reached over with her right hand and gently squeezed his left arm just like he had done to her. She had a way of being very direct, without any hesitation.

Her southern charm, vivacious manner, and playful smile performed their magic in David's heart. Although his natural tendency was to be somewhat reserved, it seemed so easy to relate to Susan. And it felt good to have such a pretty girl talk with him so warmly and comfortably. He openly mentioned Susan's "million-dollar smile" to other co-workers, and he knew inside that Susan's smile drew him to her like a powerful magnet.

As for Susan's heart, she was happier than she had been in a long time. "Yes, yes. Now I know for sure," she thought, "He *does* notice me and care about me. And he has such a gentle, pleasant manner."

Clearly, this was going to be a very good day for Susan —a day to launch a new and exciting relationship! "Who knows where this might lead?" she pondered.

Later that day, nineteen-year-old Susan got some strawberries from the produce section and ventured back to the stockroom during her break. She correctly guessed that David would be trimming vegetables there at the stainless steel sink. After some small talk, they suddenly stopped and looked at each other. Then David spontaneously kissed Susan while her mouth was still full of strawberries. And that's how their heated romance began—with the strawberry kiss.

In many ways, David came from a sheltered family background. He was the second of three children born to Barbara and Charles David Smith. A Navy veteran, his father twice served in the Vietnam war. As a devout Jehovah's Witness, David's mother sheltered him from many worldly influences as he grew up.

But David's parents did not get along. It was no secret to David that his father harbored a great distaste both for his mother and her religious faith. David found the strict practices and community isolation of his mother's religion to be distasteful.

David's first girlfriend, Christy Jennings, viewed his childhood as difficult and deprived. She invited him to her parents' home one December 25th, which turned out to be David's first experience in celebrating Christmas. "It just overwhelmed him," Christy remembers, "He was just so happy."[1] David eventually followed his father's example in rejecting the Jehovah's Witness religion. And he moved out of his parents' home in Putman, in Union County, South Carolina, to live with his great-grandmother, next door.

Although somewhat hesitant to initiate conversations with others, David was a pleasant and personable young man who valued hard work. As a student, his grades had been at least average, but he did not excel academically. It was his second nature to lend a helping hand to those around him. Others described him in endearing terms. His personality won him loyal friends.

By contrast, Susan represented just about everything that David never had. Even though Susan and David were both clerks in the same store, and they were basically on the same socioeconomic level, Susan grew up in a bigger and nicer house than David did, after her mother's remarriage to Beverly Russell, a successful businessman. She was gregarious and seemed so sure of herself. Susan earned her way to membership in the high school National Honor Society. She was voted "friendliest girl" for the school yearbook. She was regularly voted president of various school clubs. Susan was as vivacious and outgoing as David was quiet and reserved.

But inside, Susan had a burning need, a craving for male attention and male affirmation. As confident as she appeared on the outside, she didn't feel quite complete without a close boyfriend.

In their own way, Susan and David were emotionally needy people who found comfort in the company of one another.

Soon after Christy and David's dating relationship ended amicably, David began to date Susan. The chemistry between Susan and David Smith seemed to work well. One could say it worked all *too well*. Although Susan hungered for male attention and affection, her gestures, smiles, and way of touching could sometimes be interpreted by males more as a sexual invitation than a desire for close emotional communication and bonding. Whatever Susan's intentions behind her signals to David, and however it came across to him, one fact is clear: The emotional passion between them definitely grew steadily stronger by the month, until the two of them gave way to the temptations of premature sexual union. By their wedding day, David was twenty years old, and Susan was nineteen and two months pregnant.

David and Susan's relationship seemed to fulfill what each needed emotionally and held such promise for the two young lovers. But the dark hues and complex shading of pure tragedy were cast over their union from its very beginning, piling stress upon stress on the tender, delicate bond of their togetherness. Before David and Susan's marital bond could cement with time and loving attention, the emotional earthquakes of stress and grief crashed through. What began with such promise and affection was pierced with unexpected emotional pain—pain that threatened to unravel their newly found companionship from the very start of the marriage.

The unscheduled pregnancy during their courtship was the first wave of earthquake stress, a "7" on the psychological Richter Scale, but scheduling a quick marriage could partially accommodate that. Nevertheless, the stress lingered as they felt the pressures of impending early parenthood. At a time when Susan seemed to need to focus on her relationship with David, her mind also had to focus on preparing for motherhood.

Then, with little warning, David's brother Danny died on March 4, 1991, just eleven days before David and Susan's wedding day. This premature loss of Danny registered a catastrophic "9" on David's life scale for this second "earthquake." Young Danny died of Crohn's disease, a painful inflammation of the intestinal tract. Understandably, David's somber grief crowded out the normal joyous anticipation a couple otherwise experiences in the last two weeks before a wedding.

A close death in the family usually stresses a marital relationship because different people progress through the stages of grieving at different rates. This can put family members at odds with one another, being unable to understand one another's clashing emotions at any particular time. When one person is in the denial phase, the other is in the anger stage. When the first person progresses to anger, the other may have progressed to feelings of great sadness over the loss. Feeling such strong but conflicting emotions over the same loss often makes it difficult for couples to experience the level of closeness they once had. And tragically, this major stressor imposed itself upon David and Susan just days before their wedding date. Grieving a loss normally takes many months. And the months required for David to grieve over his brother were the precious early months of his marriage to Susan. Susan also experienced significant emotional loss as David moved through the phases of grieving over Danny's death. David couldn't be as available to her as he grieved, and so Susan's need for closeness to a man could not be fully satisfied.

The wedding day came on March 15, 1991, and Susan and David moved into his great-grandmother's house. To be sure, there was the initial excitement of married life together, and in a sense it really didn't matter where they were living, as long as they could be with one another.

Then, as if they didn't already have enough stress, loss, and grief to handle, three months after Danny's death, David experienced earthquake number three—the pain and anguish of his own father's bloody suicide attempt. Again, David was hit by another tumultuous "9" on the life scale of emotional earthquakes.

These three tragic circumstances affected David powerfully. The young man was not especially prone to talk much about such deeply troubling experiences. He was viewed by some as a person who holds a lot inside emotionally and keeps on working hard. One observer sympathetically referred to him as the "walking wounded."[2]

David needed understanding, emotional warmth, and trustworthy companionship. But then again, Susan had her strong emotional needs too, which seemed to be short-changed by David's attention to grappling with his father's dilemmas and grieving his loss of Danny. David's emotional antenna could not be as fine tuned to Susan's needs and desires while he was coping with his own emotional earthquakes.

It is an open question as to whether David, or any man for that matter, could have tuned in to Susan's emotional needs early in the marriage and have been able to satisfy her. This is a question we will return to later. But for now, we simply observe that, from their own perspectives, these three emotional earthquakes seriously stressed the sensitive young man, David for one set of reasons, and seriously stressed Susan, the emotionally needy young woman, for another set of reasons.

These three traumas would have been challenging for any couple to experience in their relationship, but they happened at a time that incredibly stressed the fragile marital bond before it could develop the resilient stability that could come only by sending down deep roots over a longer period of growth. Other couples can weather extraordinary stresses early in a relationship if they have the benefit of personal maturity gained by years of living, or if they enjoy the emotional support and wisdom that comes from a shared spiritual life.

Susan and David looked forward to having their baby. Julie Hart, who had worked with David's father, was pregnant at the same time as Susan. Julie says that Susan was so happy about her pregnancy that she could not wait for the baby to come. Julie kidded David that he'd have to get up at night for the baby, and David replied, "I don't mind. I'd take all the night feedings."[3]

Susan managed to work at Winn-Dixie right up until she started labor. Then, on October 10, 1991, Michael Daniel Smith entered the world, given a middle name by his parents to honor David's deceased brother, Danny. Susan wrote in her diary, "It was truly the most wonderful experience of my life. . . . He really lifted my spirits and touched my heart."

But Susan was restless. She began taking a few courses at the Union campus of the University of South Carolina. She also returned to part-time work at Winn-Dixie, with David as her work supervisor. But now, friction developed. A checkout line would be backed up, and David would look for Susan to help, only to find her socializing with another employee instead of working at her cash register. At other times, David would be irritated to find Susan flirting with her old boyfriend at the store. Friction became sparks, and sparks began to fly.

At home, the stress spilled over into regular arguments over Susan's desires to buy things David felt they could not afford. And David resented the repeated unannounced visits of Susan's mother, who seemed to have more influence over Susan than he had. Then, just two days after their first wedding anniversary, Susan took Michael and moved back to her mother's house.

David attempted to reconcile by "dating" Susan all over again during the summer of '92. During one of these dates that fall, Alex was conceived. So the couple talked seriously about getting back together for the sake of the children.

"We're going to have two babies now, and I need to feel settled in my own place," Susan said.

"We have plenty of space here for us and Michael," David told his wife, "and it's saving us a lot of money to live here."

But Susan wanted a nicer place. "I'd feel more comfortable in our own house. Can't we be planning our own place now?"

Susan pressed the issue and insisted. And she didn't want an apartment. She wanted to move up a level or so. The couple asked David's sister, Becky, and her husband, Wallace, for advice on mortgages and home ownership.

And so, in the winter of 1992, David and Susan settled on a small ranch home with a brown roof and dark red shutters on Toney Road in Union, South Carolina. The mortgage was $340 a month. Finances were not a difficulty because David was earning around $22,000 a year, and Susan earned $17,000.[4]

It is common for people to marry young and to start having children quickly in rural Union County where only 5 percent go on to college, and one-third do not complete high school. The marriage of Susan and David was like many other marriages of very young adults—lacking the maturity of years and deeply-shared spiritual resources. Their relationship turned out to be rocky and tempestuous from the very beginning. In fact, from nearly the start of their married life, family and friends say that they would never know from day to day whether Susan and David were together on Toney Road or living apart.

Most local observers say that Susan was the first to have an extramarital affair during one of their separations, shortly after Michael was born.[5] Susan resumed a romance with a former boyfriend, and David was furious! Observers also claim that David retaliated by having his own affair.

Susan and David developed a pattern of making public accusations that the other was involved in adultery, abruptly followed by making up and moving back in with one another. One day Susan would visit David at the Winn-Dixie supermarket to jealously accuse him of having an affair if he merely talked to another woman. The reported object of David's extramarital affections was said to be Tiffany Moss, a pretty young cashier at Winn-Dixie. Susan reportedly knew about it. But only a few days later, Susan would show up at the store again, this time smiling and laughing with David.

Whether Susan's dream of what marriage would be like was realistic or not, she was restless with the routines of her life with David and a new baby. The harsh realities of David's tragedies had some impact. But Susan was just not satisfied with her life and with her home.

Alex was born on August 5, 1993. But their marriage continued to go downhill.

Co-workers report that during one of the couple's separations, Susan walked in on David in bed with Tiffany Moss. Susan reacted publicly again, screaming at David, "I know we're separated, but I'm tired of you screwing around," a co-worker remembers.[6]

Ultimately, this on-again, off-again cycle crashed, and Susan and David's divorce became final in May 1995.[7] But up until the end, David consistently expressed his desire to save his marriage to Susan. He kept wanting to work on the marriage relationship, but Susan refused to give it another try, recalled a friend. This deeply upset David who believed that his boys needed their mother and father together.

For her part, Susan was observed to be a devoted mother who adored her boys. She was often seen pulling Michael in his little red wagon. In public, Michael, who was a bit on the shy side, held Susan's hand tightly. And even when separated from David, she would bring Michael and Alex by to see David at work several times a week. David would always be delighted to see his children and played with them each time.

If the boys needed anything, such as a visit to the doctor, David would always be there to help. The young parents cooperated well on matters concerning their children's welfare.

In 1993, well before her divorce proceedings started, Susan's last extramarital affair began with Tom Findlay, the flamboyant twenty-seven-year-old bachelor son of her boss, the owner of Conso Products Company.

Susan had been hired at $6.25 per hour as an assistant to the executive secretary for J. Carey Findlay, the president and CEO of Conso. The headquarters of Conso, reputed to be the largest manufacturer of decorative trim products, was located in Union, with branch factories in London, Canada, and Mexico. In this new job, Susan was exposed to the privileges of the wealthy class of society. She booked reservations for out-of-town business clients and travel arrangements for her boss, Mr. Findlay.

Susan quickly grew to enjoy working for a wealthy, powerful business executive, the head of one of the most prestigious corporations in Union. A sense of excitement returned in her life. Her opportunities there seemed limitless to a young rural girl. Susan dreamed. Susan sensed adventure. She talked with the other Conso secretaries who referred to Tom Findlay as "the catch." And Susan did what she could to catch the eye of Tom, a sure ticket to the "good life."

Then it happened. Tom asked Susan for a date. A relationship was begun, nurtured on frequent lunches and movie dates. Susan was invited to visit him at his cottage on his father's estate and participated in one of Tom's hot tub parties.

Susan's heart soared. Her hopes grew.

In legal documents in connection with the Smith's divorce, Tom acknowledged that he and Susan slept together ten times beginning in January 1994. When David discovered their affair three months later and protested, Tom and Susan temporarily stopped seeing one another. But they resumed sleeping together again in September that same year after Susan told Tom she had filed for a divorce from David.

But by now, Tom Findlay realized that Susan was much too possessive of him, and clinged to him needily. As far as he was concerned, the relationship was over.

On October 18, 1994, Tom typed his now-famous letter to Susan on his computer, explaining that he would stop seeing her because he was not ready to take on the responsibility of being a father to her two children. This letter was his reply to a card and letter Susan had sent him, apparently in the process of his continuing communication with her that they should break up.

Tom was flattering in his October 18 letter, telling Susan that she was a great person. He said he was impressed that she was in night school, and he encouraged her to continue her college studies. He said he was proud that she was working to improve her life. He expressed confidence that she would someday meet "Mr. Right." But he explained that he was not "Mr. Right" for her because he did not feel mature enough to care for a wife with two children.

Tom's letter also chided Susan for kissing and intimately fondling the husband of another Conso employee when they were nude together in a hot tub party at the Findlay estate. Tom wrote, "To be a nice girl, you must act like a nice girl, and that doesn't include sleeping with married men."

This letter arrived only four days after Susan's divorce papers were filed in court. This made Susan absolutely furious. She felt rejected again. She promptly gave Tom a stern tongue-lashing.

Tom was shocked. Could this be Susan Smith, the same sweet, soft-spoken southern gal he knew. Now Tom was certain he was smart to end the relationship.

Susan expressed agitation because she feared that David knew something that he would make public to upset her. When Tom tried to calm Susan, she lashed back with a claim that she had had sex with another member of Tom's family (a thinly disguised reference to Tom's father).

On Monday, October 24, Susan picked up Michael and Alex from day care after work and took them to Donna Garner's parents' home, for Donna to babysit them. Susan had an office appointment with a professor at the University of South Carolina at Union.

After the meeting, she and Donna went out to "Hickory Nuts," the only bar in Union. Tom Findlay was already there, talking to two women he knew. Susan and Donna sat only a few stools down from Tom. But still upset over their angry conversation the week before, Tom and Susan did not talk to one another. Susan ordered a beer. Tom told the bartender to put Susan and Donna's drinks on his tab. Susan left about thirty minutes later without saying anything to Tom.

When Susan picked up her boys at Donna Garner's parents' home, she got down on the floor and played with little Alex, kissing and snuggling up to him playfully, as the Garners recall.[8]

At noon the next day, Tuesday, October 25, Susan joined nine Conso staff members for lunch at Andy's in nearby Buffalo. Although Tom and Susan sat next to one another, Susan was unusually quiet during lunch, although the waitress recalled that everyone else was laughing and talking.

Leaving the restaurant, it was Susan's responsibility to pay the fifty dollar bill with a Conso company check. She left an eight-dollar tip. On the way back to work, Susan confided to a friend, "I've just lost the best friend I ever had."[9]

She got back to her office a bit after 1 p.m., but by 3:30 p.m. she was near tears and asked her supervisor,

Sandy Williams, if she could leave early. Sandy was the Administrative Assistant to owner and CEO of Conso Products, Cary Findlay. Sandy asked, "Is something wrong, Susan?"

"I'm in love with someone who does not love me," Susan responded.

"Who is that?" Sandy gently inquired.

"Tom Findlay."

"Do you want to talk?" Sandy offered.

"No, not now. But maybe sometime later," Susan replied. "I just need to go home now." Later, her supervisor described Susan as looking very upset.

Later, when leaving for the day, Sandy was irritated to see Susan talking with Tom Findlay at the plant. Sandy did not know anything more about Susan's relationship with her boss's son than what Susan had just told her that day.

Feeling less talkative than usual, Susan finally slipped out of the factory, this time without anything more than brief superficial chitchat with her co-workers. Walking directly to her burgundy Mazda Protégé in the parking lot, she heaved a big sigh after plopping down on the driver's seat. Preoccupied with depressing thoughts that played over and over on her mind like a broken record, she drove rather unconsciously to Carol Cathcart's day care center to pick up her two sons.

The active, sparkling eyes of her little three-year-old Michael and fourteen-month-old Alexander brightened to their fullest when seeing their mother arrive to pick them up. Alex put his little arms up in the air anticipating the usual warm embrace of Mommy, while Michael excitedly tried to describe something he had played with that day. After collecting the diaper bag, Susan carefully guided the little boys into her Mazda and snugly snapped them into their child safety seats. Then Susan drove off. As often happened, the monotonous rhythmic motion of the car quickly put the tired little boys to sleep.

Again Susan went to meet a friend at the Hickory Nuts bar, then returned to Conso. Her friend watched Michael outdoors while Susan took little Alex with her inside. Susan found Tom Findlay to tell him that she had "made up" the story about sleeping with his father just to discover how he'd react to it. This encounter only frustrated Tom who asked her to leave, saying that he'd call her later. Susan then left. She later described her feelings that evening this way: "I had never felt so lonely and sad in my entire life."[10]

Susan later claimed that she drove around town for hours that evening. Then driving along Highway 49 to the turnoff to the John D. Long Lake eight miles outside of Union, Susan paused to position her Mazda at the top of a seventy-five foot long boat ramp.

Seemingly alone in the deepening darkness of a young night, she sat clutching the steering wheel, hearing only the car engine and the heavy breathing of her two sleeping boys in the back seat. Susan had pondered this "solution" all evening, and now she finalized her decision. She slipped out of the driver's seat to stand beside the car in that partial darkness. Then she released the parking brake, and the car rolled down the boat ramp into the lake. Before it was 9 p.m., those two little boys suffered the sheer horror of awaking to the suffocating panic of engulfing water, which was totally inescapable because they were securely snapped into their car seats.

The undisputed fact was this: the very mommy that Alex and Michael desperately tried to call under that cold murky water, was the one and same villain who discarded them in such an unthinkable and cruel act. Susan caused her burgundy Mazda to become the underwater death chamber for the two precious little sons that had been born to her and their father, David Smith.

Susan's eventual confession to Sheriff Howard Wells left no doubt regarding her horrible act on the night of October 25, 1994. The big questions in the nation's mind had to do with her thoughts, emotions, and motives that dreadful night.

How could Susan have betrayed her own young children in this way? It was unthinkable, as people in Union later said. But Susan did it. And it was the ultimate betrayal. She broke the trust of her innocent little boys.

In the words of her own written confession, she sank to her "lowest point," that night, obliquely referring to her appalling treachery. But she was to sink even lower, compounding that evil deed by boldly blaming a black stranger of carjacking and kidnapping her boys still in the back seat. She deceived the country by pleading on national television for the return of her dear children.

In her double murder trial on July 20, the condition of the bodies of three-year-old Michael and fourteen-month-old Alex after their drownings by Susan was clinically described by Dr. Sandra Conradi, an experienced forensic pathologist at the Medical University of South Carolina, who had performed the autopsies on the boys' bodies at 1 a.m. on November 4, 1994. She received the bodies of the little boys still in their car seats. Neither of them was wearing shoes. After photographing them in the car seats, their bodies were taken out for the medical examination. She found no evidence of external or internal injuries or fractures in either boy. She concluded that the boys had died of drowning.

Susan's defense attorney, David Bruck, objected to having graphic photographs of the bodies shown to the jury, and objected to letting Dr. Conradi provide any graphic details of the state of the bodies, which had decomposed for nine days while Susan had deceived the nation with the lie that her children had been kidnapped. Defense

Attorney Bruck stood and said, "We stipulate that Michael and Alex did die by drowning.[11] By "stipulating," or agreeing to facts before detailed testimony, Susan's defenders were able to avoid courtroom depictions of the specific gruesome realities of what she had done.

In a matter of a few days, Susan Smith emerged from total obscurity to become internationally known through the world's news media. In high school, Susan Smith had earned her way into the National Honor Society and had charmed her peers so much that she was voted the "friendliest girl." Who would have expected her to become known as the "most hated woman in America," as one South Carolina newspaper reporter uncharitably described her after her peers in Union shouted at her, "baby-killer," "murderer," lynch her," and "stick her in a car and run it into the lake like she did to her babies." At the very least, she had committed a most hideous and unthinkable act for a mother.

The caring public still asks the heavy psychological questions:

- How could she have mercilessly murdered her own helpless little sons?
- Why in the world would anyone want to kill two defenseless and handsome little boys? and especially, why their own mother?
- What in the world was Susan thinking or feeling that awful night?
- Is there any valid excuse for this double murder?
- Did she obsess about all the males in her life who had failed her?
- Did she have flashbacks about her own father who had committed suicide in her early childhood years?
- Did the loss of her father at such a young age indirectly affect her ability to think clearly from then on?

- Did her memories of her stepfather's sexual advances distort her feelings toward males?

- Did she unwittingly transfer her rage toward males onto her own two sons?

- Did the recent letter from her lover, Tom Findlay—the one announcing his decision to end their relationship because he was not ready to become a father to Susan's two boys—have anything to do with Susan's killing her two sons?

- Did Susan want to pose as a victim with lost children to regain eligibility to receiving the affectionate interest of Tom Findlay?

- What does she really deserve? Psychiatric hospitalization? Prison time? Or the death penalty?

Can we make any sense of this unthinkable crime by delving into her childhood and teen years? Baby killing by the mother is an unthinkable crime, but then again, Susan's childhood was not entirely normal.

2

The Suicide: Was Her Mind Twisted by Her Father's Death?

"I've had it with you and all your affairs! This is just once too many times, and you're going to pay for it this time, you tramp! This gun is loaded [and] I'm going to empty it killing you and then me!" Harry's rage and paranoia were heightened by his drunken stupor. His wife, Linda, cowered and trembled at first. She then gathered her wits and boldly fled the house so she could call for help.

It was said that Harry and Linda had little in common, and their relationship quickly degenerated to arguments about sex. There was continual bickering, and they were generally not helpful to one another.[1]

Harry Ray Vaughan, a firefighter, was twenty, and his bride, Linda, was seventeen when they got married. That Linda had been already pregnant with a son from a previous relationship, did not help to establish trust between the newly married couple.

With Harry, Linda gave birth to her second son, Scotty. Then a little girl was born to them in Union on September

26, 1971. They affectionately named her Susan Leigh Vaughan. But by then, this young couple's marriage was already "on the rocks." The Vaughan family lived just outside downtown Union, in a modest brick house on Siegler Road, near Foster Park Elementary School where the children eventually attended.

Marital conflicts continued to escalate to the point that Harry became increasingly violent, threatening to kill Linda and himself. Harry's alcohol problem strongly contributed to his dysfunctional family relationships. He became obsessed with Linda's alleged marital unfaithfulness. Then on yet another occasion in Linda's home, Harry took a gun and threatened to kill Linda and the children.[2]

All this turmoil made Susan's older brother, Scotty, very frightened in his own home. And when Susan was yet a preschooler, her oldest brother Michael made an attempt to hang himself. He was treated at Duke University Medical Center and at another residential treatment facility, according to courtroom testimony.[3]

On the other hand, Susan, being the youngest, was not as keenly aware of all the marital conflict as were her brothers. But the turmoil must have come through to Susan in a more obscure, unconscious way, because she became a sad little girl.

The mother of one of Susan's little playmates described Susan at age five to be quite different from other little children: "She was unusual . . . an unhappy child. Not that she never laughed. [But] attending a birthday party . . . Susan would stare in space, like she wasn't there."[4] Susan was regularly observed to be like this.

But Susan was the "apple of Harry's eye." She would simply "light up" whenever Harry entered the room. She rapidly developed an especially close relationship with her daddy. She felt better when she was with him.

After seventeen years of marriage, Linda Vaughan filed for divorce. The divorce became final on December 7, 1977, when Susan was only six.

It could be an understatement to say that Harry was absolutely devastated by the breakup of his marriage and by being forced to live apart from his children, Scotty and Susan, and Linda's Michael. He reluctantly moved into an apartment in a nearby Union housing development and began to make frequent visits to a local bar called "Alias Smith & Jones" where he would socialize and drink heavily.

The bartender there later described Harry as "outgoing," "good-looking," "sweet," and "a nice guy."[5] But as Dr. Seymour Halleck testified during Susan's trial, the community was not really aware of Harry's depression, alcoholism, occasional violence, and severe marital conflicts. Only those closest to him could detect that something could be wrong. Dr. Halleck observed:

In Susan's family, [there was] an effort of family members to try not to appear depressed. Like Harry Vaughan—people didn't see him as depressed, but he killed himself.[6]

Susan was exposed to the tragedy in a traumatic manner. One morning, Linda called her co-worker and neighbor, Iris Rogers, and said she would be late. This was unusual for Linda, and she asked Iris to baby-sit little Susan in her home nearby. Iris watched little Susan, and later brought her back home. There were cars in front of the house, and the front door was unlocked. Iris then let Susan go into the house, and Iris went back home.

Later, Iris was told that no one was at home when she dropped Susan off. Susan stayed alone in the house for several hours that evening until the family returned to give her the tragic news: Daddy died.

Susan was not told, at first, that Harry committed suicide. Instead, her mother only told her that Susan's daddy was cleaning a gun and the gun accidentally went off,[7] and that "Your daddy went to be in heaven." Little six-year-old Susan pondered this news for only a brief time before she came to a child's conclusion: "I want to go to heaven, too, so I can be with my daddy."

It was only when she was older that Susan learned what actually happened: Five weeks after Harry and Linda's divorce became final, Harry came to Linda's house and made some threatening statements once again. Harry took Scotty. A uniform crime incident report, dated January 15, 1978, indicated that Linda H. Vaughan phoned a complaint against Harry to the Union city police at 2:42 a.m.

When the police arrived at the house, they heard a man and a woman angrily arguing. Then Linda pleaded, "Help me." Officer Smith went to a side door and found a broken window pane and glass all over the floor. He also saw Harry strike Linda.[8]

The officer demanded to be let in, and Harry complied. It was obvious to the police officer that Harry had been drinking. Then Harry was burdened with enough concern about himself that he uncharacteristically went to the magistrate and tried to have himself arrested for fear that he might harm someone.

At 4:30 that same morning, something of what Harry feared happened: In the depths of his despair and hopelessness, Harry took a gun between his legs, aimed at his abdomen, and pulled the trigger.

But he didn't die immediately. Lying on the floor in a pool of his own blood, it is possible that Harry changed his mind about wanting to die after he felt the pain of his self-inflicted wound. This is not an unusual reaction for people who make suicide attempts, as Dr. Seymour Halleck made clear in Susan's trial. At that time many people living in Union felt that Harry had not actually intended to kill himself but intended to dramatically draw attention to his emotional anguish in the hope of somehow being reunited with his family. In any event, after he shot himself, Harry reached for the phone and was able to call 911 to ask for emergency medical help.

The Union city police officers, responding to the call, came to the door but found it locked. They could hear Harry call for them inside and could see him lying wounded on the floor. They broke a window and were able to enter to get him. They raced him to a hospital for emergency surgery. But tragically, Harry died in the hospital of what was determined to be a suicidal attempt.

Harry was only thirty-four years old at the time of his death, and Susan—his dear little Susan—was yet a tender young girl of only six years of age. She had lost the daddy she adored.

Susan yearned for her special, warm relationship with her daddy. Harry's passing left a huge void in her life. She keenly wanted that close father-daughter relationship to which she had been accustomed. Little Susan sorely missed her father, Harry.

Throughout her childhood years, Susan kept her father Harry's old coin collection and an audio tape of his voice in her bureau drawer.[9] Once in a while, she would take that audio tape out to play it. She felt warm inside when she heard Daddy's voice, but at the same time, it made her feel even more sad to feel his loss.

Shortly after Harry's suicide, Susan rather instantly acquired a stepfather. Her mother quickly married Beverly Russell. Bev had several daughters from his previous marriage, and now the blended family moved to a much larger house in the exclusive Mount Vernon Estates in Union.

Bev was the wealthy owner of a downtown appliance store in Union. A state Republican executive committee-man, he was a prominent and well-known person in Union, as well as a member of the advisory board of the Christian Coalition.

Gradually, Susan began to compete for her new step-father's attention and affection, but not always very suc-cessfully. Susan perceived herself in competition with her mother for Bev Russell's attention. But we'll come back to Susan's "solution" to this dilemma later. At this point, we can note that Susan and her two older brothers were de-scribed as being emotionally close to their stepfather.[10]

What Were the Effects of Susan's Biological Father's Absence On Her Development?

We can only piece together the facts as revealed in Susan's trial with what we know about girls as they grow up from psychological research studies. It's much like a complex puzzle that can be assembled to reveal a fuller picture. There is much we know from research on little girls who have lost their fathers, research that traces their development into young adult life. Such studies can help us to understand the life of someone like Susan. Much of this research was conducted by Dr. Mavis Hetherington, a psychology professor at the University of Virginia. Profes-sor Hetherington studied girls who lost their fathers by death, girls who lost their fathers by divorce, and girls who grew up with both their mothers and fathers through all their child and teen years. She interviewed these girls, observed them interacting with peers at school events, and gave them and their mothers numerous questionnaires every year until they had grown from young childhood into young adulthood. Here is a summary of what she found.[11]

The young girls who lost their fathers due to death, grew up with a "larger than life" image of their fathers. They idealized their memories of their daddy, and had idealized views of men in general. They didn't blame their fathers for leaving them—they thought, "It wasn't Dad's fault that he died; he didn't want to leave me."

In their high school socials, these girls were observed to be shy around the teenage boys. Compared to the other two groups of girls, these girls took a "standoffish" approach to boys, spending more time in the ladies' room. They were more likely to stand around the edges of social events, observing and admiring boys rather than interacting with them.

These girls eventually married at older ages compared to the girls with fathers and the girls who lost fathers by divorce. And they tended to marry men who were more educated and wealthier than they were.

By contrast, the young girls who lost their fathers due to divorce (with infrequent visitation from the fathers), grew up with a negative image of their fathers. Before their father departed, they loved their daddy, but when he left, they took it personally in some respects, feeling rejected by him. They tended to blame their fathers for the divorce and for leaving them. They thought, "It was Dad's choice that he left, so he must have wanted to leave me."

These girls also have low opinions of men in general—they feel that males generally are "louses" who will inevitably disappoint you. And yet, they yearn for male attention, male approval, and male affection. They develop a cynical attitude toward males: "You can't live with them, but you can't live without them."

In their high school socials, these girls were observed to "throw themselves" on the teenage boys. They were observed to be the most aggressive girls in approaching boys and in physically touching and hugging them in social settings. They were more likely to place themselves right in the center of the boys' attention at social events.

These girls who had lost their fathers by divorce had the highest rates of teenage pregnancy and out of wedlock births compared to the girls with fathers and the girls whose fathers had died. These girls eventually married at younger ages than the other two groups of girls, and they tended to marry men who were more likely to be high school dropouts or only high school graduates with no college education.

The third group of young girls who grew up with both a mother and a father, developed neither an idealized nor a "larger than life" image of their fathers. Instead, they had a more balanced, realistic perspective of them as men with some virtues and with some faults. They developed the same "realistic" view of men in general.

In their high school socials, these girls were observed to be neither shy nor overly forward around the teenage boys, on the average.

These girls eventually married at ages in between the later ages of the girls who lost fathers by death and the early ages of girls who lost their fathers by divorce.

At first, because Susan only knew that her father died and "went to heaven," she would not have experienced Harry's departure as his rejection of her. From what we can put together at this time, Susan's first reactions were to cling tightly to her memories of her father and to wish that she could also go to heaven to be with "Daddy." If anything, she would have idealized him.

Eventually, Susan learned that her father died by his own hand. Thinking through what suicide means, she came to the realization that her father chose to die. It is but a short leap from there to think, "he chose to leave me here without him." Thus, Susan grew to experience her father's departure as a form of rejection of her.

Susan's English teacher, Deborah Green, at Union High School recalled an incident involving Susan on a school field trip to Presbyterian College. Deborah stated in court that she will never forget the incident. Susan could not hide her depression that day. At one point, Deborah thought Susan was with another adult, Donna, and Donna thought Susan was with Deborah. When Deborah and Donna connected again, they realized that Susan was missing. Knowing that Susan had been depressed and that she had previously revealed a suicidal attempt at age ten, Deborah feared the worst.[12]

But Deborah found Susan wandering about by herself. Deborah could see that she was crying.

"Susan, what are you doing over here?" Deborah asked gently. *"Susan looks like a little child,"* Deborah thought.

"I've been walking around," Susan explained half-heartedly.

Deborah compassionately put her hand on Susan's arm, "Sit with me here on this bench." Deborah could see that Susan was terribly troubled.

"Nothing in my life is right," Susan complained, "I just want to die."

Then Deborah feared that Susan had been looking for a way to commit suicide.

"Tell me about it," Deborah urged.

"I feel deserted. I feel my daddy just couldn't have possibly loved me or he wouldn't have killed himself,"[13] Susan blurted out with a gush of new tears.

Deborah attempted to reason with Susan, and it seemed to calm her down. She spent a great deal of time with Susan in an effort to help her emotionally.[14]

This perception of her father left her with strong mixed feelings, which a little girl cannot very well understand. What was the emotional effect of feeling, "Daddy left me. My daddy rejected me." Susan's feelings of self-worth took a nose dive. A huge emotional need to be close to daddy was unfulfilled. A gaping hole existed in her heart. And with feelings of low self-worth came stronger feelings of abandonment, sadness, and, yes, even depression for a young girl.

In a tragic sense, Susan lost her father, first by divorce, and then by death, a self-inflicted death. Her growing up experience ended up paralleling the lives of Professor Hetherington's group of girls who lost their fathers by divorce, because Susan experienced her father's suicide as a rejection of her.

Before her father departed, Susan loved her daddy, but she tended to blame her father for leaving her. She thought, "It was Daddy's fault that he left; so he must have wanted to leave me. I wasn't good enough for him to want to stay here with me."

Susan also grew up with a low view of men in general. But she wanted to please males. Like the girls in Dr. Hetherington's research, Susan developed the cynical attitude toward males: "You can't live with them, but you can't live without them."

In her high school years, Susan was quite outgoing with the boys. She "threw herself" at adult men and boys her age. Consider David Smith's earliest "up close" look at Susan:

> It was in the store. She was surrounded by three or four guys. They were from high school, younger

than she was, and they were all laughing and making small talk as she checked through their purchases . . . she was all smiles, especially to men . . . .
I think it would be easy to take her wrong; it would be easy to take her as being flirtatious.[15]

Socially, she could, in some respects, be described, as "throwing herself" at the teen boys. She was popular and at ease in approaching boys and in physically touching and hugging them. Girls with this psychological background were more likely to place themselves right in the center of the boys' attention at social events. Consider again David Smith's observations of her as a fellow employee at the Union Winn-Dixie supermarket:

Susan had a pretty complete romantic life . . . .
As soon as she started in at Winn-Dixie, I began hearing rumors about her affairs with people who worked there.
People said she was seeing not one but two of her co-workers.
People would notice the way she and this guy hung all over each other all the time, were always huddled up together, talking, how they stayed in the office late at night after the store closed . . . .
She was actually spending the night with this older beau.[16]

Remember that Dr. Hetherington found that the girls who had lost their fathers by divorce had the highest rates of teen pregnancy and out of wedlock births compared to the girls with fathers, and the girls whose fathers had died? Like the first group of girls, Susan twice became pregnant in her teen years before she was married.

In her senior year in high school, at age eighteen, Susan was secretly dating an older fellow employee at Winn-Dixie and became pregnant; she quietly had an abortion.[17] At the time, Susan got herself into further trouble because she also dated another fellow employee and had sex with him. Her older romantic partner found out about it, and Susan ended up being hospitalized at the Spartanburg Regional Medical Center from November 7 to 15, 1989, for medical and psychiatric treatment for taking a non-lethal overdose of aspirin and Tylenol® in a suicidal gesture. The doctors in that hospital found out that this was not Susan's first suicidal attempt. She had also taken an overdose of aspirin back when she was only thirteen years of age.

Only a short time after her hospitalization, Susan began to date David Smith, and David recalls that they had sexual intercourse on their second date, followed by a habit of having unprotected intercourse.[18] Not surprisingly, Susan's second unwed teen pregnancy was therefore fathered by David (while David was engaged to another girl). This time, Susan decided to accept twenty-year-old David's desire for marriage, and delivered her son, Michael, seven months after their wedding.

Like the girls who lost fathers by divorce, in Dr. Hetherington's study, Susan married at a younger age than the mean age of girls with fathers who died, and girls with biological fathers through their teen years. Further resembling that research group, Susan married a fellow who was only a high school graduate with no college education. So we are beginning to see that Susan's life was following the pattern of millions of other females who have lost their fathers in childhood in a way that they perceived the loss as some kind of rejection by that father.

Did Susan's father's suicide cause Susan to develop a mental disorder in her adult years?

We can consider the courtroom testimony of psychiatrist Seymour Halleck who performed a psychiatric evaluation of Susan after her crime for the defense attorney's case.[19]

Dr. Halleck's study of the family history of Susan Smith, combined with his psychiatric interviews with her, led him to conclude that Susan had a tendency to depression since childhood. In fact, Dr. Halleck concluded that the family tree of Susan has a genetic loading for depression because so many of her relatives had symptoms of depression or alcoholism. The courtroom testimony of a family friend, Iris Rogers, described Susan as an unhappy child at age five before her father committed suicide. So Susan was already a child prone to depression even before Harry Vaughan committed suicide.

We have seen that her father's suicide was enormously stressful on Susan while she was yet a young child. It was also a major personal loss to her which she, in turn, experienced as a form of rejection.[20] So, indirectly, her father's suicide was a contributor to her propensity to become depressed. Even with a genetic predisposition to becoming depressed, one often needs the addition of a psychosocial stressor to activate that predisposition.

There are hundreds of psychological studies that indicated that life stressors place a person at greater risk for mental disorders. [21] Bereavement over a death in your family is a most severe stressor.[22] Susan's father's death, then, would well be a significant stressor on her that could trigger Susan's greater genetic tendency toward depression.

Did Her Father's Suicide Make It More Likely That She Would Attempt Suicide Herself Later in Life?

Psychological research studies have found an increased risk of suicidal gestures[23] and suicide[24] in people following the death of their parent. In Susan's case, the relationship between her father's suicide and her own reported attempts at ages 13, 18, and 23, is not a direct cause. Instead, it is an indirect influence.

Susan's father's suicide was experienced as a stressor by Susan, a suicide that helped trigger her likely genetic tendency to depression. This condition led her to be depressed at times. But Dr. Halleck also concluded that Susan developed a Dependent Personality Disorder (which we will discuss more later), and this disorder in combination with a depression could contribute to her suicidal thoughts.

At Susan's trial, her first cousin, Lee Page Harrison, testified about her close, almost "sister-type" relationship with Susan as they were growing up. Susan had no sister, but Lee was just a little more than one year younger than Susan and lived just five houses down the street from Susan's family. Lee showed the jury some snapshots of childhood experiences with Susan, pointing out some sadness in Susan.

Lee testified that Susan's two suicide attempts in her teen years "both scared me." "I never understood it," she said. Lee noted that Susan covered up her troubles well by her smiling. In retrospect, Lee thought Susan "hid her pain well."

James William "Billy" Shaw, Jr., a certified counselor who works for the Union schools, gave courtroom testimony about the visits Susan made to him when she was a student.[25] Starting at about the age of thirteen, Susan made multiple visits to Mr. Shaw's counseling office at school. Susan's P.E. teacher, Sheri Jackson, also told Mr. Shaw about Susan's apparent depression.

Shaw described Susan as a despairing and angry person. There was a particular incident he recalled when Susan was angry because her stepfather would not let her watch certain TV programs.

Shaw reported that when Susan made her suicidal gesture at age thirteen, he considered it ". . .enough to be a
cry for help." He admitted on the stand that he did not
feel that he had gotten to the bottom of Susan's problems.
However, he did not feel her problems were severe
enough to warrant a referral to a mental health expert. He
felt that he and Susan's involved teachers could provide
the emotional support that Susan seemed to need.

Studying Susan's history during his forensic evaluation
in 1995, Dr. Halleck had a more serious interpretation of
Susan's unhappiness and suicidal tendencies at age thirteen. He described Susan as then "thinking obsessively
about suicide." Susan wrote a suicide note and told her
teachers that she wanted to be in heaven with her father.
She also reported to Dr. Halleck that she took aspirin daily
with a false belief that she could gradually kill herself that
way. Differing from Mr. Shaw's assessment, Dr. Halleck
asserted that, if Susan had come to his emergency room at
age thirteen, that he would have hospitalized her in a psychiatric unit or placed her in an intensive psychotherapeu-
tic treatment program.

In short, Susan was more likely to experience suicidal
thoughts after experiencing her father's death by suicide.
But there were other psychological factors, in addition,
that combined to make the temptation of suicide a repeated experience for Susan. So we do see an indirect relationship between the suicide of Susan's father when she
was a little girl of six, and Susan's later mental problems
with depression and her desire to commit suicide to go to
heaven to be with her father.

In her opening statement of the double-murder trial,
one of Susan's defense attorneys, Judy Clarke, portrayed
Susan as a loving but immature and troubled mother who

could not cope with life, "and she just snapped." In painting this portrait of Susan, Clarke stated that Susan was devastated by her father's suicide, and thus, "into her teens, she was sort of a walking wounded. She learned to put on a sweet and happy face."[26]

Susan's loss of her biological father by suicide left an emotional vacuum and a feeling of being rejected by her father. It also placed her at higher risk for attempting suicide herself. But this alone is not enough to explain why she killed her own sons. Could her victimization by her stepfather's sexual abuse provide the psychological key for discovering why she killed her precious little sons, Michael and Alex?

3

The Incest: Did Sexual Abuse Cause Her Mental Illness?

"My heart breaks for what I have done to you," wrote Beverly C. Russell, Jr., in a letter to Susan Smith on Father's Day, June 1995. Susan was in prison awaiting her double murder trial, and the letter was from her step-father. "I want you to know that you do not have all the guilt for this tragedy . . ." the letter continued.

"Of course, had I known the result of my sin, I would have mustered the strength to behave according to my responsibilities. Many think that my failure had nothing to do with Oct. 25, but I believe differently. I failed you, Linda, God and the rest of my family."

As Bev read from his letter in a hushed courtroom on July 27, 1995, he did not look at Susan at the defense table who was bowing her head. Susan's mother dabbed her eyes.[1]

"My remorse goes way beyond sorrow for getting caught or exposed, which is significant in itself," Bev struggled to continue reading as he tearfully choked back his emotions. "But to see unfolding before our eyes the principle of reaping and sowing, to lose Michael and Alex, to see you in prison, to see Linda crushed with extreme loss, to lose a whole family relationship, and to hurt my children, and all you needed from me was the right kind of love."

Instead, Beverly Russell confessed that he had given his teenaged stepdaughter a sexual relationship. With his voice interrupted by tears and cracking with emotion, Mr. Russell dramatically described how he had "crossed the line" when his hugs became sexual caresses, when his fatherly kisses grew sexually passionate and deep, and when he took the hand that meant to hold his fatherly hand and moved it to touch his genitals.[2] He then convinced Susan to conceal the truth about their relationship and to keep it a dark secret for nearly a decade. As a result of his repeated failure as a father, Mr. Russell felt strongly that he had warped Susan's life and became an important factor in her dreadful decision to roll her car with her children into John D. Long Lake on October 25, 1994.

With this reasoning Mr. Russell pled with the jury to spare Susan's life. "Susan was sick," Russell said. "Even though she loved her children, what happened was from a sickness . . . It's horrible. We can't get onto grieving for Michael and Alex because we're so focused in on trying to save Susan's life."[3]

As you recall, Susan's mother had divorced Susan's biological father, Harry Vaughan, and married a local businessman, Beverly C. Russell, Jr., in 1979. Bev became "the force that held the family together" according to Susan's older brother, Scotty. Russell also rose to a prominent leadership position in the South Carolina Republican Party and the Christian Coalition.[4]

But Bev's accomplishments in business and politics were of little consequence to little seven-year-old Susan.

To her, Bev was more importantly her new "daddy." He couldn't really replace Harry as Susan's beloved father, but year by year, Bev's affirmation became increasingly important for Susan. Without realizing why, she longed for his attention and approval, but it sometimes seemed that he gave more attention to other family members, especially Susan's mother, Linda.

One day in 1987, just shortly before Susan turned sixteen, Bev's daughter from his previous marriage came to stay overnight. She was given Susan's bedroom, and Susan was to sleep on the family room couch. Bev was relaxing on one end of the couch when Susan came in that evening.

Much like she did when she was a little girl with her daddy, Susan crawled into Bev's lap to go to sleep. Now this behavior for a fifteen-year-old is unusual—it is like a fifteen-year-old acting like a little five-year-old. Perhaps crawling into Bev's lap seemed provocative to Susan's stepfather.

Susan closed her eyes, relaxed, and fell asleep. Gradually, she awoke to the awareness of Bev's hand moving slowly but firmly from her shoulder to her breast.[5]

Bev then moved Susan's hand and placed it directly on his genitals. Susan continued to pretend to be fast asleep through all this. Later she told her mother that she did not object or jump off his lap because she "wanted to see how far he would go." Susan's explanation sounds manipulative and is clearly inappropriate.

But Bev's behavior was one hundred times more inappropriate. We can assume that Bev knew better, and later he confessed to the wrongness of his sexual advances toward Susan.

Susan swore out a complaint in the Fall of 1987, a complaint that was investigated by the South Carolina Department of Social Services and the Union County

Sheriff's Office.[6] Linda Russell obtained the name of a family counselor from the school guidance counselor. The family went for counseling four or five times before quitting, according to a statement made to the police.[7]

We know that Bev's sexual abuse of Susan was wrong. Yet, at the same time, several questions can be addressed in terms of what is known from psychological studies. That knowledge can inform us about the psychological implications of sexual abuse for Susan. The following questions are important:

- What are the typical psychological effects of child sexual abuse upon the female in her adult years?

- Are the effects different when the sexual abuse occurs in the later teen years, as in Susan's case, compared to an earlier childhood onset of the abuse?

- Did Susan Smith develop the common reaction of a Posttraumatic Stress Disorder as a result of experiencing sexual abuse as a late teenager?

- Was Susan's teen behavior provocative, sexually tempting to the stepfather? If so, would that affect her emotional reaction to the abuse?

- To what extent was the sexualization of the stepfather/daughter relationship "mutually consensual," and would that alter the emotional effects later? Can a sixteen-year-old truly "consent" to sexual interaction with a stepfather, or is there an automatic coercion factor by virtue of the stepfather's authority status and age?

- Could the sexual abuse/relationship between Bev and Susan be one of the causes of her mental illness?

As we have seen, Russell was active in both the Republican Party and the Christian Coalition at the time the sexual abuse took place.[8] And, incredible as it seems, one of these sexual abuse incidents reportedly took place on the same evening that Russell had put up "Pat Robertson for President" posters around town.[9]

Susan had discovered that she could get Bev's attention by being sexually provocative. Susan was developing an attraction to Bev, more as a lover than as a father figure. She felt in love with her stepfather and saw their relationship as "an affair." In this way, psychiatrist Seymour Halleck viewed Susan as assuming "a responsibility that never belonged to her."[10]

But she had internal conflicts about her sexual involvement with Bev and sometimes felt guilty about it. Her sexual experience with Mr. Russell "increased her guilt, and diminished her self-worth as a person; and all those contributed to chronic depression. . . .[The sexual molestation] made her more guilt-ridden and depressed, and depression [was] related to [her] suicidal [thoughts]."[11] In Dr. Halleck's words, "The striking thing to me was that she blamed herself for it. She felt responsible and treated it as her responsibility. This is part of her . . . self-punitive [nature]."[12]

Was the sexual abuse of Susan her fault? Dr. Halleck was asked this question while he was on the witness stand in Susan's double murder trial. "I do not believe a grown man could not be responsible. . . . The burden is on the person in control. And the person in control is the adult," he replied.[13]

After the Department of Social Services became involved in the case, Bev agreed to move out of the family residence. But the family was in turmoil since Bev's sexual abuse of Susan was reported to the Family Court. Though the family received some counseling for a short time, Susan later reported that the abuse never completely stopped.

"The family seemed to blame [Susan] as much as Bev," commented psychiatrist Seymour Halleck. The Russell family was concerned that the report of the sexual abuse might spread, and they blamed Susan for making the situation public by her reports of abuse to the school staff.

In February 1988, Susan went to her guidance counselor, Camille Stribling, to complain about being sexually molested by her stepfather. It was the second time he had molested her. By law, the school officials were required to report the allegations, so Stribling called the South Carolina Department of Social Services, and an official there contacted the Union County Sheriff's Office.[14]

The sheriff's records indicate that in March 1988, Susan reported an instance of sexual molestation by her stepfather to her high school guidance counselor and to her mother, Linda Russell. Linda reported to the legal authorities that Bev had not denied the incident when she had confronted him about it. The South Carolina Department of Social Services sent a caseworker to interview Susan, her guidance counselor, and a few of Susan's teachers.

The caseworker testified at Susan's trial that she learned that Bev Russell, on repeated occasions, had fondled Susan's breasts on top of her clothing, French-kissed her with an open mouth, and had put her hand on his genitals.

The social worker also testified that "Susan was very concerned that the family would fall apart. She assumed the full responsibility herself." The social worker counseled Susan that she had done nothing wrong and that such incestual sexual relations were the adult's responsibility, not the minor's responsibility. The social worker also explained to Susan that she would "try to keep the family together."

When the same social worker interviewed Mr. Russell, he acknowledged that "Susan [had] told the truth." "He felt very responsible for what happened," the worker testified. "He was glad I was there, and he felt a weight had been lifted from his shoulders by telling me."

In the presence of Mr. Russell's attorney, Mr. Guess, Linda Russell, the sheriff, a deputy, and Susan, three options were given the family: 1) Mr. Russell could leave the home, 2) Susan could leave and stay with relatives, or 3) Susan could be sent into foster care.

The charges possible against Mr. Russell would be "assault and battery of a high and aggravated nature" or "lewd act on a minor." But because there had been no penetration, and Susan had been under sixteen years of age at the time, the usual charge would be "assault and battery of a high and aggravated nature." Legally, there is no "age of consent" for incest in South Carolina, according to courtroom testimony in Susan's case. Because this meeting lasted until 9 p.m., a visit to the family was scheduled for the next day to obtain a formal statement for law enforcement.

But the next morning, when the social worker and detective were scheduled to visit the Russell family to obtain a formal statement to launch charges against Bev, the detective simply informed the social worker, "We are not going to the Russell home because the investigation is closed." The social worker disagreed, contending that the sexual abuse was criminal in nature. Though Mr. Russell was a very prominent member of the community, the social worker felt that "all people should be treated equally." She also said in court that "I felt pressure was put on Susan to drop [the complaint.]"

For whatever reasons both Susan and her mother decided not to press charges against Bev.

Unwilling to give up at that point, the Department of Social Services case worker notified Assistant Sixteenth Circuit Solicitor Jack Flynn in order to obtain a court order to pursue the case. Mr. Russell's attorney, Robert Guess, was able to come to an agreement with Solicitor

Flynn, and this understanding was presented to Judge David Wilburn who sealed the court records on March 25, 1988.[15]

When the social worker was asked about this order in Susan's trial, she testified, "That was the only order I heard sealed in twenty years."

When girls who are sexually abused do not receive strong emotional support from their mothers, they are more likely to react with stress.[16] When we consider this finding with the facts in the Susan Smith case, we notice that Susan told several people about her father sexually abusing her. She told her mother. And she told several school employees, including counselors. But unfortunately, her mother may have persuaded her to not press legal charges against Bev Russell, and her mother did not keep Bev out of the house. Several interesting questions could be asked:

- Did Susan perceive this as lack of support from her mother? Probably.

- Did Susan feel abandoned by her mother in this? This is entirely likely.

- Did Susan feel unprotected by her mother? That would be a logical conclusion.

- Did Susan perceive an implied endorsement by her mother of Bev's sexual relationship with her? That is possible as well.

Tragically, the facts that came out of Susan's trial suggest that there was minimal support for Susan from her mother in this matter of Susan's sexual abuse. In this sense, some view Susan as a victim of both Beverly Russell and her mother, Linda Russell.

When she was sixteen years old, Susan complained

again about her stepfather's spying on her and suggested inappropriate sexual advances. Susan had asked Bev to bring her a towel as she stepped out of the shower, even though she already had a towel with her.[17] Again, this brief story suggests that Susan provoked her stepfather, but we still need to hold Bev entirely responsible if this alleged incident contains truth, and if Bev reacted sexually to Susan in response.

In another incident recorded by police, Bev returned from posting signs for presidential candidate Pat Robertson and appeared in Susan's room. "He was standing over her and he kissed her and then took her hand, thinking she was asleep, and put her hand on his genitals and he kissed her again," the police report stated. [18]

Various sources now indicate that Susan must have given conflicting descriptions of her sexual relations with Bev. So even with courtroom testimony from a number of individuals, it is unclear what went on sexually between Susan and Bev.

A news item in the Charlotte *Observer* reported that Susan told a psychiatrist in 1989 that she was happy with her sexual interaction with Bev because she was jealous of all the attention he gave her mother. Susan insisted that sex with Bev was a mutually consensual "affair," and that it began when she was only fifteen. The *Observer* also reported that unnamed sources stated that Bev admitted his sexual relations persisted with Susan until about six months before the murders of her two children.[19]

According to Mr. Russell's own testimony on the witness stand, during the penalty phase of Susan's double murder trial, he admitted that his incest with Susan began when she was a teenager and persisted into her marriage to David Smith. He described his sexual relationship with Susan as occurring primarily in his home in Mount Vernon

Estates in Union, once in Susan and David's house, and once in Spartanburg. In fact, he said their last sexual episode occurred in August 1994, just two months before the murders of Michael and Alex.[20]

During Susan's trial, James Logan, the Senior Agent of the South Carolina State Law Enforcement Division testified that during his interrogation of Susan, she told him that she and her stepfather had "emotional ties." SLED Agent Logan reported, "He (Mr. Russell) used to come in when she was pretending to be asleep." Tom Findlay (one of Susan's extramarital lovers) testified that Susan told him that she was fearful that her estranged husband David would disclose her affair with Beverly Russell, which continued into her adult years.

As these details started to leak out to the community, some family members vociferously defended Bev against the molestation allegations. But Bev Russell has broadly acknowledged inappropriate behavior toward Susan in a recent interview with the press. "I am responsible for and ashamed of what happened. I appreciate the fact that some of my friends and family have tried to speak up in my defense. But they don't know what I did. I am finally getting the professional help that I needed."

After this sexual abuse became public, Bev and Linda separated with Bev moving in with an aunt in February 1995. Mr. Russell also abruptly resigned from the state Republican Executive Committee, explaining that for personal reasons, he could no longer function in that capacity.[21]

Sexual abuse by stepfathers is much more common than sexual abuse by biological fathers. This is true, partially, because the parents who care for intimate physical needs of infants and preschoolers (such as feeding, chang-ing diapers, bathing the infant) rarely develop any tempta-tion to view that child as a sexual object. Most stepfathers were not present during those early childhood years, but enter the picture often after the girl is older or post-pubescent.

There is a range of long-term effects of sexual abuse that occur to girls as children or as teenagers. When the abuse occurs during a girl's adolescent years, it can be especially confusing as to her feelings about her own role in collaborating with the abuse.

Even though the adult perpetrator is one hundred percent responsible under the law, the teenage girl can experience paradoxical emotional effects of the sexual molestation. At first, she may feel flattered, excited, and aroused by the sexual attention. But then feelings of anxi-ety, guilt, and shame may appear.[22]

This may be true especially when the daughter is required to deceive her mother about the abuse that is occurring with the father-figure. The girl can experience guilt for the deception and for colluding with the wicked deceit insisted upon by the father-figure. She can learn to be manipulative in this way because it is a taught "survival technique," as a social worker testified in Susan's trial on July 22, 1995. In Susan's case, this experience of enforced lying, tutored by her stepfather, could have been a power-ful temptation for her to lie at times when she was embar-rassed about what she had done, as she did, in fact, in so many other relationships.

The most expensive of all Susan's lies was the story that a black man carjacked her Mazda Protégé with her two little boys in the back seat. That lie cost the combined governmental agencies involved a total of over two million dollars for the nine day search. The cost of her trial plus costs to imprison her will doubtless cost more than one million dollars more.

The strong emotions caused by sexual abuse have been found to impair a girl's development of self-confidence. Normally, the mid-adolescent period involves the development of a "diffused identity" in which key roles are acquired with parents, peers, school, and others.[23] This allows for the growth of normal self-confidence. But sexual abuse often interferes with this process, doing damage to an individual's sense of self-esteem. When a damaged sense of self-esteem is combined with social stress in the absence of supportive relationships, a girl may develop depression.[24]

Crucial identity tasks are disrupted in adolescence when sexual abuse is imposed on a girl. There is serious psychological damage to the girl's ego when the perpetrator is a father figure.[25] There is also a loss of a sense of security and protection, which is a normal role for a father to provide a child. The trust between parent and child is broken. Research has found that the result is a disturbed self-concept in the abused girl which is associated with a lower self-esteem. The integrity of her body image is damaged, and she can become prone to be disgusted with her own female body. These psychological dynamics induce self-defeating behavior patterns in the girl who may be prone to degrade herself with sexual promiscuity.[26] She may continue to seek love and approval through sexualizing her subsequent relationships with males.

When the sexual abuse is repeated over a prolonged period of time (for many months or years), or if the sexual abuse occurs only once but in a violent manner, the girl can later develop a mental disorder, such as depression, substance abuse, or a "Posttraumatic Stress Disorder."

Posttraumatic Stress Disorder is a mental disorder in which the person persistently re-experiences a traumatic event, persists in avoiding reminders of the trauma, experiences a numbing of general responsiveness, and experiences increased arousal (sleep disturbance, irritability, concentration problems, hypervigilance, or exaggerated startle responses). Usually, the original traumatic event involves death, injury, or a grave threat, which was experienced or witnessed. But the traumatic event can be a violent personal sexual assault, or in children, inappropriate sexual experiences without threats, actual violence, or injury. The disturbance lasts more than one month, and causes significant distress or impairment in daily living. Studies of lifetime prevalence vary in their findings from one percent to fourteen percent of the population.

But during Susan's trial, the various doctors who testified did not find a "posttraumatic stress disorder" in her case. That Susan's sexual relationship from the teen years was "consensual" in Susan's eyes, may very well be the reason why this common disorder found in sexual abuse victims was not found in Susan's case.

However, another disorder that results from sexual abuse was identified in Susan's case—a dissociative process. When forensic psychiatrist Seymour Halleck testified about his evaluation of Susan while she was in prison, he noted that at times she was not aware of all aspects of a situation that she was in. Dr. Halleck referred to this process as "dissociation," a clinical term which describes a mental process which prevents certain experiences or memories from entering consciousness because of the intolerable anxiety linked with that experience or memory.[27] As a result of dissociation, this unconscious psychological process functions rather independently of the rest of the individual's personality.[28]

But Dr. Halleck also clarified that with respect to her actions on the night she let her car roll into the John D. Long Lake with her boys inside, that "she could have conveniently said that she ran from the car and felt detached, but she didn't. There were no dissociative episodes at the time."

In her trial, Susan Smith's defense lawyers brought witnesses to the stand to provide evidence regarding her earlier allegations of sexual abuse by her father to gain sympathy for their client in the sentencing phase. Dr. Halleck informed the court that there was a number of effects of sexual abuse, including poor self-concept and interference with the capability to have normal gratification in sexual relations later as an adult. He noted that Susan "[was] sexually active, but it [was] rarely pleasurable for her."[29]

Susan, according to Dr. Halleck, did not derive sexual pleasure from being sexually involved with her stepfather. Instead, "she felt her skin was crawling after sexual contact with him, but she did it anyway."[30]

Susan's last lover, Tom Findlay, was cross-examined by Susan's defense attorney, David Bruck. "Let me ask you about the intimate relationship you had with Susan. Was she very aggressive?"

"No, sir," Tom politely replied.

Bruck became more specific, "Was she sexually aggressive?"

"No."

"Sex-crazed?" Bruck inquired.

"No."

"Was she driven sexually?"

"No. What Susan got wasn't physical pleasure, but the feeling [of being] needed, loved, being cuddled," Tom explained.

Dr. Halleck's evaluation concluded that Susan's sexual experience with Mr. Russell contributed to her approach to men. She sought to please them. "She gives gifts to men. She rarely asked men to do anything sexually for her.

She continued to [have sex] to please men. She often had sex with David in hopes of keeping him."[31]

Dr. Halleck also diagnosed Susan as having a "dependent personality disorder," describing her as a person who "feels she can't do things on her own. She constantly needs affection and becomes terrified that she'll be left alone."[32] Dr. Halleck further claimed that Susan "has as severe a dependent personality disorder as I have ever seen." He observed that Susan seeks many men and then feels depressed.

On July 20, during the Smith trial, I was interviewed on a national television show and was asked, "Does there seem to be anything unusual about Susan's postures and nonverbal behavior?"

I noted the testimony of law enforcement personnel at the trial who described how Susan regularly appeared to be acting during the time she lied to them and to the nation, claiming that a black man had kidnapped her two sons. One investigating officer, Agent David Cadwell, testified that when she made sounds like crying, often there were no tears. Sometimes Susan would lower her head when appearing to cry, "but if she managed to work up some tears, she'd raise her face, as if trying to be sure I noticed."[33] The absence of tears was also noted in the testimony of FBI Agent David A. Espie III, who called it "fake crying," that he had seen used by some criminal suspects to buy time in an interrogation while they thought of what to say next.[34]

Clearly, Susan Smith was a victim of sexual abuse, and her sexual abuse contributed to her tendency to become depressed and to her greater temptation to become involved in sexually promiscuous relationships. But it takes much more than sexual abuse as a teenager to lead to murdering one's own children.

The chief prosecutor, Tommy Pope, cross-examined the Department of Social Services social worker who worked on Susan's case, and clarified that this state office no longer handles a case after the child reaches the age of eighteen. The law then assumes that the legal adult is henceforth responsible for his or her own actions. Until age eighteen, the adult is held legally responsible for sexual interaction with the minor, even if the girl is the "sexual aggressor."

But Susan desired a continued sexual relationship with her stepfather during her adult years until she was taken into custody for suspected murder. In the state of South Carolina, an official license is required for any sexual relationship to be legal—the marriage license. There is no provision for legalizing "consenting sexual relations between adults," other than a legal marriage. Therefore, the continuing sexual relationship between Mr. Russell and Susan Smith after Susan turned eighteen years of age meant that both of them were then breaking the law.

The mental condition of Susan Smith was important in determining the guilt of Susan in regard to the murders to which she ultimately confessed. If the individual is legally sane, as Susan's defense attorneys admitted, then the person must 1) perform the intention to kill, and then 2) voluntarily perform the murderous act. In Susan's case, she assumed the "I'll be God" attitude of intending to take another person's life. In court, Susan's expert psychiatric defense witness admitted that Susan had intended to kill herself and her children, and that she made that choice voluntarily.

No psychological research, however, demonstrates that sexual abuse *causes* the "I'll be God" attitude of intending to kill another human being. No psychological research demonstrates that sexual abuse *causes* a person to perform murder.

The twelve member jury convicted Susan Smith of double murder. That is, those twelve people were unanimous in judging the facts presented in court and concluded that Susan had evil intentions and voluntarily chose to kill her own sons.

The extent of sexual abuse of minors in the United States is significant. There are approximately 400,000 cases of sexual abuse reported annually in the United States, which is now close to 15 percent of all reports of child abuse.[35] The best research on prevalence rates indicates that 1 in 3 girls in the United States are sexually victimized as minors. But 1 in 3 mothers do not kill their children. These statistics explode the "abuse excuse."

Susan's sexual abuse by her father became a root of her later adjustment problems and tendency toward depression, but it takes more than depression to prompt a mother to kill her own children.

So we need to ask: Did Susan also develop an evil life pattern of deception and manipulation to get her own way, which set her on a collision course with her own children?

4

The Infidelity: Did Susan Become a Manipulative Deceiver?

During the summer of 1988, between her junior and senior years in high school Susan worked as a cashier at the Winn-Dixie supermarket in Union.[1] During that time, she was romantically involved with two of her co-workers, one of whom was a married man. They would be seen talking together regularly, and Susan was seen "hanging all over" one of the men while at work.

By the next summer, after Susan had graduated from high school, she would tell her mother that she was working the "third shift" at another job although she was actually spending the night with this older married man. But if that were not exciting enough, Susan began sneaking behind the back of this lover to be with yet another man who also worked at the same store.[2]

When the two men discovered that they both were sleeping with Susan, the man who had had the longer affair with her became angry. He arranged to have his newer competitor transferred to another Winn-Dixie grocery store, in another county in South Carolina, to get rid of him.

With one remaining lover at the store, Susan began driving out to his home when his wife was at her job. But when her lover's wife discovered the affair, she went to the store with their children and sarcastically said to Susan, "I see your baby's working tonight." Fed up with Susan's two-timing and realizing that his marriage was about to break up over his affair with Susan, this man requested a transfer to a different Winn-Dixie store away from Union, and told Susan their relationship was over.[3]

Susan reacted to this crisis by swallowing a nonlethal dose of Tylenol® as a suicidal gesture.[4] She was hospitalized at the Spartanburg Regional Medical Center.

Recall that Susan's sexual relationship with Bev Russell, which began with sexual caresses when she was fifteen, continued into her adult years as a full-fledged affair until August 1994. Her affair with her stepfather thus overlapped her marriage to David Smith. Susan described her sexual liaison with Bev to Dr. Halleck as an "affair." She described mutual feelings of attraction between the two of them. Susan would usually meet at Bev's home for sessions of extended mutual caressing and oral sex.

In the fall of 1994, Susan worked full-time, took a part-time course load at the University of South Carolina in Union, had custody of her two preschool boys, and carried on sexual relationships with Bev Russell, Tom Findlay, and with her separated husband, David. She grew increasingly anxious, and when alone, she easily became depressed. She began taking days off from work and started drinking, which was unusual for her. Then she had some problems with her girlfriend Susan Brown.

Susan Brown, the Marketing Manager for Conso Products, knew Susan Smith from a distance in her high school years. It wasn't until they worked together at Conso that they began to really get to know one another and to become friends.

At one point, in late 1993, Susan Smith made a request of Susan Brown, "Could you possibly include me in your group of friends here at work?"

"Of course I can, Susan. I'd be happy to," replied Susan Brown.[5]

"I like Tom Findlay," Susan Smith confided, "and he's in your social circle. That's why I want to be included in your group."[6]

In early 1994, Susan started a sexual relationship with Tom Findlay. It was interrupted for several months after Tom discovered that Susan was still married to David. But after Susan informed Tom that she had filed for divorce from David, Tom and Susan resumed sexual intimacies. But by October 16, Tom made it clear that he wanted to back away from a romantic relationship with Susan, to be "just friends."

The new friends, Susan Smith and Susan Brown, decided at work that they would have dinner together on Thursday evening, October 20, 1994. The two women picked up Alex and Michael from day care and met David Smith, who had agreed to be with the children that evening.

When the two women got to the restaurant, they saw a group from Conso and decided to eat with them. Smith and Brown returned later to Susan's home, and, about that time, David returned the children to their mother. As the two Susans chatted, Alex became upset, wanting to play with a yardstick that his mother thought would be too dangerous for him. Susan Smith put the yardstick on the top of the refrigerator. She turned to Susan Brown and said, "I wonder what life would be like if I didn't have kids. I married so early in life."[7]

On Sunday, October 23, 1994, Susan Smith went to see Tom Findlay in the hope of restoring his romantic interest in her. She was afraid, however, that he would still be upset with her for kissing and fondling a married man while participating in a nude "hot tub" party at Tom's place. She had also told him about her sexual relationship with Bev Russell to gain his sympathy. But that only seemed to turn him off.

Susan was very worried what David was going to do with his new knowledge of her multiple sexual affairs. Things were getting too complicated. She had too many "secret" relationships, and they were starting to become known in dangerous ways by the wrong people, and the relationship she longed for the most was unraveling before her eyes.

Back at Conso, it was unusually cold in the office. Susan Brown complained, "I'm getting a bit cold. I'm about to shiver."

Tom Findlay kindly offered help. "Let me get my sweat shirt for you. It's over in my studio." Tom brought over his Auburn University sweat shirt.

Later, when the office had warmed up enough that Susan Brown no longer needed the sweat shirt, she returned it to Tom's drafting table.

A short time later, Susan Smith came over to Susan Brown's desk and commented, "It's cold in here."

"Oh, I've got just the solution for you! Tom has his Auburn sweat shirt in his studio. He loaned it to me early this morning, and I put it back after I was through with it. I'm sure he wouldn't mind if I went and got it for you to wear," Susan Brown volunteered.[8]

Susan Smith would later return the sweat shirt to Tom. It would be her last act of manipulation of her former lover. She was trying once again to achieve the love and acceptance that seemed always to elude her.

At the time of the murder of her boys, Susan was working full-time, studying as a part-time university student, functioning as the custodial parent of her two preschool children, socializing several nights weekly at Hickory Nuts Tavern, and carrying on affairs with at least two men, plus enticing David to have sex. Something was shortchanged in this self-absorbed lifestyle, and that something appeared to be the boys, according to David's observations of how frequently she left the boys in other people's care.

Susan's habit of becoming involved in multiple sexual relationships seemed always to create a major volcanic explosion for herself or for one of her relationships. October 25, 1994, was one of those days for Susan.

Tom testified that Susan attended a work-related lunch that had been arranged to entertain a co-worker from the Conso Products London factory who was visiting Union on business. Susan sat next to Tom Findlay. She "didn't say much" at that lunch meeting, according to Tom's recollection.

Once Susan returned to her desk, Sandy Williams returned to her office after having conducted some company business in Charlotte, North Carolina. Sandy immediately noticed Susan's tears while she struggled to work. Susan was an assistant to Sandy who served as the Administrative Assistant to the Conso Products president, Cary Findlay. Sandy needed to be updated on anything that came up while she had been on her Charlotte business trip. But the first thing Susan told her had to do with Susan's personal life. "I'm in love with someone who doesn't love me."

"Who?" Sandy inquired.

"Tom Findlay. But it can never be because of my children," Susan complained with no further elaboration. Susan offered no other reason for her failed prospects with Tom other than her children.[9]

Then around 2:30 p.m., Susan called Tom on the office phone to ask him to step out on the front lawn at Conso to speak with her on their break. Susan went outside to a picnic table where she met Tom, her recently estranged lover. There, Susan told Tom that her estranged husband, David, was threatening to make public some details that would prove to embarrass her (and by implication, could embarrass Tom and his family as well).

Susan was in tears. "David knows some information."

"What information?" Tom inquired.

"That I supposedly cheated the IRS, and the fact that I had an affair with a family member of yours," Susan replied.

"A family member of mine?"

"Yes, with your father," Susan replied coyly.

"What? My father? You've got to be kidding," Tom said.

"No, I'm not. I had an affair with your father," Susan insisted.

"Susan," Tom finally replied after recovering from the momentary numbing that this shocking news had on him, "you can rest assured that our friendship will not be changed by this information. But at the same time, you must understand that this just confirms that our intimate relationship will have to stop forever."[10]

After talking a little longer, Tom excused himself. "Susan, I really need to be getting back to work now."

When Susan returned to her desk, it was clear that she had been crying. Sandy Williams noticed that her mascara was running down her face. Susan remained obsessively preoccupied with trying to regain Tom's romantic interest. She stewed on her dilemma as she tried to work. But tears welled up in her eyes as she panicked about their relationship. She felt abandoned by the man she had come to love. He wanted "just friendship" when she wanted to regain the romantic and sexual intimacy they had shared on ten occasions that year. She just had to talk to Tom again, she thought.

Approaching her supervisor, Sandy, Susan made a request in a manner implying that she would not be productive anymore that day. "I just need to go home now."

Caringly, Sandy asked, "Do you want to talk?"

"No, not now," was Susan's instantaneous reply.

"Well, then, you can go home now," Sandy generously consented. Susan next went to Tom's photography studio at the Conso Products plant sometime around 4:30 p.m. that same afternoon.

"Tom, I'm still very upset," Susan said with tears. Susan handed Tom his Auburn University sweat shirt. "Here, I need to give this to you because I may not see you again."

Interpreting the comment as a threat that she would take her own life, Tom kindly replied, "No, Susan. You take it and wash it." Tom meant to communicate his concern, and to discourage Susan's implied suicidal thought.

Susan took the sweat shirt back, but she was still in tears. Tom tried to comfort her. "Tomorrow will be a different day."

Then Susan left to pick up her kids at Carol Cathcart's day care center. She headed toward the Hickory Nuts Restaurant and Tavern, and found Susan Brown driving from work going in the same direction. She tailed her, waved so Susan Brown could notice her in her rearview mirror, and when Susan Brown caught on, she pulled over and parked. Susan Smith looked very concerned and earnestly asked Susan Brown to do her a favor. "Would you come with me back to Conso to watch my kids for a few minutes while I talk to Tom Findlay?"

"Okay, I can do that."

"Oh, thanks so much! I really need to talk to Tom as quickly as I can because I played a practical joke on him and I need to explain. I need to tell him I was just kidding before he gets too upset."

"Oh, I see."

"And one more thing. Can you vouch for me when we get there that I was just playing a practical joke on him when I said I had an affair with his father?" Susan Smith asked.

"Now, Susan, I have to work with both you and with Tom, so I prefer to keep out of any personal things between the two of you. Besides, I don't know anything about this. I'll be happy to watch Michael and Alex for you, but please leave me out of your conversation with Tom."

By the time Susan returned again to Conso, it was around 5:30 p.m. Sandy Williams was just leaving work and saw Susan Smith in the employee parking lot. Sandy felt manipulated and deceived by Susan who had insisted that she could not stay at work and had to go home. But Sandy did not say anything; she just let it go. Later in court, Sandy explained, "I was annoyed. She left work early and then came back to Conso. I saw that she had the children with her."

Susan probably didn't notice her supervisor, Sandy. She just proceeded to walk over again to Tom's studio, this time holding little Alex, while Susan Brown tended to Michael.

Susan knocked at Tom's door. He opened it with a surprised look on his face. "Why are you here, this time, Susan?" Tom asked with a puzzled look on his face.

"Tom, I'm sorry. I just [feel] I have to tell you right

away. I was playing a practical joke on you when I told you about sleeping with your dad."

Tom looked even more surprised.

Susan turned to Susan Brown, "Isn't that right, Susan. Tell him it was all a practical joke."

Shocked that Susan Smith would drag her into it after she had just told her she wanted to stay out of a personal matter that she knew nothing about, Susan Brown immediately responded with a very polite, but firm businesslike tone, "I really don't know anything about what you're saying, Susan. It would be best for us all if I just stay out of this whole thing." Then Susan Brown turned, took little Michael by the hand, and stepped back a few paces from the studio door.

Tom was totally confused now. Why was Susan saying all these strange, contradictory things. "I'm just glad our intimate relationship is over. Boy, did I make the right decision," Tom thought.

"Susan, why did you tell me this story in the first place?" Tom finally sputtered.

In a normal demeanor, Susan replied matter-of-factly, "I just wanted to see how you feel about me."

Tom was stunned. Over the past couple of weeks, he had carefully explained all his reasons why their intimate relationship was over, and why they could still be friends nonetheless. He had even detailed his thinking in a letter to Susan the week before. And Susan did this stupid trick, "to see how you feel about me." *"I feel totally confused by this woman,"* Tom thought. *"And she even brought Susan Brown to give some kind of credibility for her changed story."*

Then Tom explained to Susan, "I don't really feel it's at all appropriate to discuss such things right there in front of your children and Susan Brown. I'm sorry, this is just not the time to talk." Further, Tom still had company work to finish and needed to get back to it. As Susan left, he thought, "This is getting more and more strange. And this was the third time Susan demanded my time today."

Now Susan seemed a little upset, a little shaken. But she wasn't crying like she was earlier that afternoon. She was a swirl of emotion. She yearned to restore her intimate, romantic relationship with Tom, but everything she had tried that day had failed.

Back at her car, Susan Smith had tears in her eyes. She confided in Susan Brown, "I feel I've lost Tom as a friend."

Susan Brown comforted her and tried to help her think more realistically, "No, I think you and Tom will continue to be friends."

Seeing that Susan Smith was in tears, Susan Brown offered to spend time with her that evening. "Susan, I could go out to a movie with you this evening. My husband is spending time tonight shooting pool with a friend."

"No, not this evening. I'm okay. You just go ahead. But if I need you, I'll let you know," Susan Smith replied.

Later that evening, Susan Brown was eating dinner at Hickory Nuts with several friends, including Tom Findlay. During dinner, a waiter brought a cordless phone to Susan Brown.

"Hello."

"Hey, Susan. This is Susan Smith. Is Tom there?"

"Yes," replied Susan Brown. She didn't need to search the restaurant to give a reply because, in fact, Tom was sitting right beside her.

"Has he said anything about me?" Susan Smith inquired with somber earnestness.

"No, not at all."

"Is Tom mad at me?" Susan Smith inquired, in a normal voice, apparently no longer crying.

"No," replied Susan Brown, because, in all honesty, Tom hadn't said a word about Susan Smith there in the restaurant. Susan Brown didn't really want to get into an extended conversation there with Susan Smith about Tom, as Tom was sitting next to her, so she gracefully found a way to exit the phone conversation.

The next time Susan Brown talked to Susan Smith was the next morning after Brown heard of the reported abduction of Michael and Alex. Susan Brown went over to the Russell home to console Susan. Susan appeared very upset, and as she looked at some photos of her boys, she said, "Oh, my God, what if my children don't look this way the next time I see them!"

Then, out on the driveway, Susan Smith told Susan Brown the story about the kidnapping at the red light at Monarch. She asked Susan Brown as she left, "When you speak to Tom, could you tell him that I asked you to have him call me? Tell him he doesn't need to worry about David being here."

This time was like the many other times that she felt panicked that things weren't turning out how she wanted them to. As before, Susan got herself tangled deeper and deeper in her own web of deceit.

What did Susan want? Both as a teenager and as an adult, Susan consistently wanted her own way and sought to get male affection through any device she could think of.

What did Susan do to get all the male affection she craved? She lied. She connived. She manipulated people and circumstances. She betrayed those she said she loved. But she got repeatedly tripped up in her lies with her lovers and later with her own husband.

Susan was a sexually unfaithful marriage partner, and yet she filed for divorce on the grounds that her husband,

David, was allegedly having an affair. Susan was again posing as a victim, a continuation of a lifelong pattern.

Despite early press reports, the story eventually came out, according to the testimony of Tom Findlay himself, that Susan had been having an affair with him around the time she filed for divorce. Living in a small brick house with two preschool children and a $17,000 secretarial salary, Susan "saw Findlay as her ticket out of the working class."[11]

Just hours before the death of her boys, Susan had a series of meetings with Tom Findlay, first to tell him she was sexually abused by her stepfather, Beverly Russell. When that failed to elicit his sympathetic affection, she went to see him again, this time to get his attention by telling him that she had once had sex with Tom's father, Cary. When that news turned Tom off to her, she convinced a friend to accompany her (trying to get her friend to vouch for something she knew nothing about), to tell Tom that she had only been lying when she said she had an affair with his father.

For all the brevity of her adult years of freedom, Susan accumulated tawdry sets of sexual exploits and entanglements with both married and unmarried men. This series of meetings with Tom Findlay on October 25, 1994, demonstrate Susan's manipulative ploys and her motivation to get what she wanted from a man, using any degree of deception and disregard for the truth. Prosecutor Tommy Pope pointed to such manipulation to show Susan as the type of person who would do anything to get her own way.

Susan developed an evil pattern of deception and manipulation to gratify her emotional pleasures. This set her on a tragic collision course with her responsibilities to care for the well-being of her children.

But many people are deceptive and manipulative in relationships without killing their own children, so did Susan actually become insane to commit that unthinkable crime?

5

The Betrayal: Was Susan Evil or Insane When She Killed?

In her opening statement to the court, Susan's defense attorney, Judy Clarke, contended that mental illness affected Susan's actions.

> You need to know about the life of Susan Smith so we must bring you back. . . . That night on her way to her mom's, she was terribly upset. She was dealing with fear . . . and turmoil. . . . She was at the lake for this purpose. . . . It was wrong and she knows there is no excuse.

Attorney Clarke elaborated on how Susan's father had committed suicide because her mother did not live with him anymore.

> Susan tried suicide twice before October [1994]. Suicide was an option to her. Suicide is why we are here.

What, in fact, did Susan want? The prosecution lawyers —Tommy Pope and Keith Geise—presented evidence indicating that Susan wanted to escape her loneliness, unhappiness, and stress by establishing an exciting, intimate relationship with the wealthy Tom Findlay, free of the stresses of motherhood. After all, the weeks before and the day of the crime, Susan was frantically preoccupied with how to win back the romantic affections of Tom, and he had made it clear that her two boys were an obstacle to their relationship becoming closer and more permanent.

Just one week prior to the boys' deaths, Tom had written his now famous letter (quoted later in its entirety):

> . . . there are some things about you that aren't suited for me, and yes, I am speaking about your children. I'm sure that your kids are good kids, but it really wouldn't matter how good they may be— the fact is, I just don't want children. These feelings may change one day, but I doubt it. . . . I don't want to be responsible for anyone else's children. . . .[1]

So what did Susan do? She killed her two sons and promptly reported them kidnapped.

That same evening, David Smith testified that his wife did something that struck him as very odd. David drove to their home on Toney Road to retrieve some personal items to bring to Susan's mother's home where Susan and David planned to stay while the search went on for their children. Completely out of the blue, Susan turned to David to say, "I hope you won't get mad if Tom Findlay comes to see me at Mama's house."[2]

"Our kids were gone, and I didn't care if Tom Findlay or anybody else came to see Susan. Our kids were missing and my focus was on finding the kids," David testified in court on July 25, 1995.[3]

The cold hard fact established by the jury is that a troubled Susan Smith confessed to single-handedly drowning her two sons, three-year-old Michael and fourteenth-month-old Alex, on October 25, 1994, in John D. Long Lake, seven miles northeast of Union, South Carolina. The angry public perception was reflected in a response heard on a television talk show when a viewer said, "She drowned her sons like rats."

But at the same time it is also true that the facts of her childhood and teen years indicate that she was a sad victim of her parents' divorce, her biological father's suicide, and sexual abuse by her stepfather.

But when David Smith was asked by Barbara Walters on ABC-TV's "20/20" if his ex-wife might be something of a victim of her childhood that included her father's suicide and her sexual abuse by her stepfather, David forcefully replied,

> Not in the slightest chance. If you're sexually abused, if your spouse cheats on you, that does not give you any reason to murder your children. Nothing can justify what she done.[4]

So which is it?

- Did the tragic events of Susan's early childhood and later teen years produce uncontrollable emotions of depression with associated mental confusion which darkly clouded Susan's usual sense of right and wrong, rendering her incapable of controlling her actions?

- Should Susan be excused as a psychological victim of her environment who is in desperate need of psychotherapy, not punishment?

- Or is Susan a coldly calculating, sinful woman who sought to manipulate her circumstances to obtain selfish extramarital gratification at the expense of the innocent lives of her own helpless little boys?

• Did Susan kill her own children to rekindle romantic attention from her boyfriend Tom Findlay?

• Did Susan kill her boys to vent her rage against her estranged husband, David?

• Is Susan a responsible moral agent who deserves the ultimate punishment from the justice system?

In short, was Susan insane or sane at the time on October 25, 1994, when she killed her little children?

It is interesting to trace the views of Dr. Seymour Halleck who performed a psychiatric evaluation of Susan Smith and testified for several hours concerning his findings. In a dramatic moment in Susan Smith's double murder trial, her defense attorney quietly asked Professor Seymour Halleck, "Is Susan an easy read?" Dr. Halleck firmly replied,

No. She has an incredible need to please and make everybody feel better. She focuses on what makes you comfortable, not on what's inside [her]. It is very difficult to get at who Susan Smith is and what she experiences.

In retrospect, it would not be unusual for Susan to have felt sad as a young six-year-old girl as she grieved her father's death. It would not be surprising if Susan felt sad about her experiences of rejection by the numerous males she pursued in the years just prior to and after her marriage to David. But were her reactions normal sad emotions or grief that accompanies a loss or an unfortunate experience of rejection? Or were her reactions extreme enough to warrant a diagnosis of a clinical depression?

Forensic psychiatrist Seymour Halleck interviewed Susan Smith while she was in jail for nearly six hours on February 23, 1995, for two hours on March 23, for three hours on June 13, and for a little over three hours on July 7. Then, in the hushed courtroom, Dr. Halleck sat confidently in the witness chair and testified, in a forceful voice, about Susan's story in his sworn courtroom testimony:

> I made assessments on how she sees herself. . . [and] how she sees herself as different from what she wants, how she relates to people, [and] how she sustains relationships.
>
> [I looked for] the way she puts thoughts together, looking for [any] problems in thinking. . . . I also looked for feeling tone, her moods of the moment.

Then Attorney David Bruck asked Dr. Halleck: "Did you take Susan's word for what she told you?" The doctor replied,

> No one is perfect in telling when a person is lying. But a difference in forensic evaluation [compared to] clinical evaluation is that you approach it with doubt and cynicism. [I] look for denying and malingering.

Then Dr. Halleck testified as to what he found in his evaluation:

> She often said that . . . she hears voices that say she's doing good, and other voices saying she's doing bad.

These could have been auditory hallucinations . . . a classic symptom of schizophrenia. [But] I asked her, "Do these voices seem real or just thinking in your head?"

She said, "Dr. Halleck, these are not voices but arguments I'm having with myself."

In further testimony, Dr. Halleck noted that from his review of the material from psychologist Dr. Arlene Andrews who had testified at Susan's trial prior to him, he concluded,

There is a very high incidence of mental illness in members of her family, [a] high genetic loading for depression. . . .

The bottom line is, having this kind of family tree increases threefold that she will get depressed.

So, was Susan depressed at the time of her crime? Did she experience normal sadness, a "major depression," a "dysthymic disorder," or another form of clinically diagnosed depression?

Dr. Halleck conceded that few persons knew that Susan Smith was depressed for two reasons:

First, she was very good at covering it up.

Second, when her loneliness is satisfied, her depression diminishes. If there's a threat to her relationship, then she gets depressed again.

Her depression is atypical, in that at times she felt okay.

She would look normal most of the time except for when she broke down [crying]. In the community, she would control herself.

Frightened of being alone, she needed constant

stimulation. She [needed] to have somebody to talk to.

The worst time [was] at night when the TV [was] off and there [was] no one to talk to.

Then on the night of the crime, Dr. Halleck provided a vivid description of Susan's mood and thoughts:

> As she is driving, she is constantly crying. Uncharacteristically for her, she turns off the car radio. She finds her body shaking uncontrollably. She feels nauseous. During that one-hour drive, she bit her nails off completely.
>
> She's driving, thinking that she has to kill herself because there is nobody around who cares for her. She feels she's lost everybody.
>
> . . . she almost ran off the road because she's shaking and so distressed.
>
> She finds a bridge over Broad River and contemplates jumping and taking the kids off [with her]. But Michael is crying so she decides not to.
>
> The main thought she had was that she had to die. Before she got [to the John D. Long Lake], she felt that she had to take the kids with her. . . because she was concerned they would live without a mother.
>
> She sets the hand brake. Then releases it. Then she pulled it up again. Then [she] got out of the car [and let it go]. . . All this is irrational. She was not thinking rationally at that point. With her strong religious convictions, she firmly believed that the children would go to heaven.

Straying again from the microphone, her attorney David Bruck leaned forward slightly and dramatically asked, "Why didn't Susan go into the water?" Dr. Halleck replied:

> I can only reach the assumption that when she ran out of the car, that her self-preservation instincts took over, and although up to that moment she fully intended to kill herself, she got frightened.
>
> It is unclear if she remembered her children were in the car. With her level of anxiety and despair, it's possible she blocked out the awareness.
>
> She's given me several stories on this, so I conclude she really doesn't remember.
>
> She often [gave] me the answer, "I must have known the kids were in the car."
>
> Then other times, she [said], "I couldn't have known [the kids were in the car].
>
> I don't know if she had full awareness if the kids were in the car. I don't think she [knew].
>
> By the time she came to the top of the ramp, she knew the kids were in the car. She ran screaming, and couldn't see the car. Then she [was] fully aware the kids [were] in the car in the lake.

When asked, on the witness stand, if it's possible for people to be capable of not thinking of something they knew just a moment earlier, and to apply this to Susan's situation at the lake, Dr. Halleck replied, "It's possible. People are capable of blocking things out. I can't use the word probably."

Dr. Halleck repeated: "When she ran out of the car, her self-preservation and survival instincts took over. It is unclear if she remembers her children were in the car. With her level of anxiety and despair, it is possible she blocked out awareness of the children." Dr. Halleck testified that Susan gave several stories on this so he concluded that she really doesn't remember. Further, he believed that since she gave him the self-incriminating answer, "I must have known the kids are in the car," on some occasions, but said at other times, "I couldn't have known the kids are in the car," that she doesn't know herself. Dr. Halleck himself said he doubted if she remembered at the time if the kids were in the car.

By the time she came to the top of the ramp, she knew (if she didn't know before) that the kids were in the car. Then she ran screaming and couldn't see the car anymore. Then she is fully aware of the kids being in the car in the lake.

As she ran up the hill, she thought about what she would tell people. "People will hate me; people will not understand." As she was running up the hill, she was making up the story. I think at this point her self-preservation instinct took over. She went to the house and told the story.

It is credible to me that a story with so many loopholes could have been made up while running up the hill.

She was very intent in finding ways to kill herself, but had no access to weapons. She was never alone. She was caught up with the lies she was telling and was terrified with what would happen if she had to tell the truth.

"I have no reason to doubt her account. She has consistently not lied and not tried to portray herself as a sympathetic person. From the beginning of the interview she portrayed herself as a bad person, as a hateful person.

"She's in unusually bad circumstances now and that factors in [to how she feels now]. I warned that she needed to be watched more carefully. With my concern for her depression, I thought she should have antidepressant medication. She seemed calmer on the medication, including sedatives, but more depressed. In July she looked a little more lively, less sedated. On each occasion I saw her, she said if she had the means to kill herself, she would.

It's so consistent with her history. I see it as a continuing manifestation of her illness.

"She told me the last time I saw her. Prozac made it harder to cry. She feels somewhat better on it, but still suicidal. {Her response to Prozac} supports the condition of depression.

"If she had been treated with medication earlier, she would never have killed the children. I have a very strong opinion that the intent was suicide."

On cross-examination by Tommy Pope, counsel for the prosecution, Dr. Halleck conceded, "She's capable of trying to save her life and let her kids die."

Dr. Halleck testified that he characterized this incident on October 25, 1994, as an "aborted suicide attempt." But he also conceded that Susan had told him that she had intended to kill her children too. When directly asked by Mr. Pope, "She had prior intent to kill the kids?" Dr. Halleck replied, "Yes, along with herself."

When Dr. Halleck described how he believed that Susan had a prior intent to commit suicide that evening and "to take the children with her," Pope carried out his dramatic and memorable line of questioning:

Pope: If I kill myself, it is called suicide, right?
Dr. Halleck: Correct.
Pope: Now, if I decided to commit suicide and "take you with me," would I have to kill you?
Dr. Halleck: Yes.
Pope: Is it possible for me to "suicide" you?
Dr. Halleck: No.
Pope: If I killed you, would it be called murder?
Dr. Halleck: Yes.
Mr. Pope asked again, "She affirmatively chose to kill Michael and Alex?"
Dr. Halleck replied, "Yes."

"Did she understand right and wrong?" asked Mr. Pope.

"Yes. . . She knew it was criminally wrong to kill her children, and she chose to do it," Dr. Halleck responded.[5]

Defense attorney David Bruck asked Dr. Halleck to provide his diagnosis of Susan Smith, and the doctor said that she had many of the features of a "Major Depression," However, he explained that her symptom pattern did *not* technically satisfy the diagnosis of a "Major Depression," according to the commonly accepted diagnostic system used by doctors called the *Diagnostic and Statistical Manual of Mental Disorders*, Fourth Edition.[6]

How does this manual describe a "Major Depression?" Major Depression, as described in this manual, is a disorder in which a person experiences a change in their prior functioning *for at least two weeks*, during which they have either a depressed mood (feeling sad, empty and "blah," tearful, cranky or irritable) or a marked loss of interest in normal activities ("not caring any more"), plus at least four of these additional symptoms of depression:

1. a significant increase or decrease in body weight or appetite;
2. difficulty in sleeping or oversleeping;
3. observable restlessness or slowing down in activity;
4. fatigue or loss of energy;
5. feelings of worthlessness or inappropriate guilt;
6. difficulty in thinking, concentrating, or decision-making; or
7. recurring thoughts of death or suicidal thoughts and/or suicide attempt.

These symptoms occur *most every day* in the absence of drugs or medical condition, and the depression is at a level

that causes significant distress or impairment in functioning in everyday situations. Normal grieving may result in
many of these same symptoms, but does not constitute a
major depression if it lasts no longer than two months.

Studies indicate that in adolescence and adulthood,
Major Depressive Disorder occurs two times more frequently in women than in men. Various studies have
found a lifetime risk of Major Depressive Disorder to be
between 10 percent to 25 percent for women and between 5 percent to 12 percent in men. Some have called
depression the "common cold" of mental health because it
so commonly affects so many people.

Dr. Halleck could not give Susan a diagnosis of Major
Depression because she never experienced a depressed
mood "for at least two weeks." Instead, Dr. Halleck reported that Susan was only depressed when she was alone.
She almost always had a normal mood when she was
around people. Working full-time and having her two children and her social life, she never had two weeks of depressed mood.

Dr. Halleck thus gave her the "leftover" diagnosis of
"Depressive Disorder Not Otherwise Specified." He further explained that Susan seemed to have an "intermittent
depression."

Another diagnosis that Dr. Halleck did not find to
apply to Susan was "Dysthymic Disorder." Dysthymic Disorder is characterized by at least two years of having a
depressed mood for more days than not, together with
additional symptoms of depression, which are not as numerous as in a Major Depression. Dysthymia is characterized by a less severe depression, which is chronic over a
number of years. The person may feel inadequate, uninter-
ested in life, withdrawn, guilty, irritable, or angry, and may
also brood over the past or be less productive. The lifetime
prevalence of Dysthymic Disorder is 6 percent of the

population, and in adulthood, women are two to three times more likely to have dysthymia than men.

The diagnostic category that Dr. Halleck did apply to Susan, "Depressive Disorder Not Otherwise Specified," is a "leftover" category that includes depressive symptoms that do not meet the full diagnostic criteria for Major Depressive Disorder, a Dysthymic disorder, or an Adjustment Disorder with depressed mood. It can include premenstrual dysphoric disorder, or more minor depressions, or depression in conjunction with some other condition.

Psychological research by Dr. Constance Hammond at U.C.L.A. has shown that women with depression often contribute to their own depression by the way that they interact with their environment. A case could be made that Susan's dysfunctional relationships with men contributed to her own propensity to become depressed. In fact, Dr. Halleck also gave Susan the diagnosis of a Dependent Personality Disorder, claiming that she was the most dependent person he had ever evaluated in his psychiatric career spanning about forty years.

Certainly, Susan's marital difficulties, her higher financial aspirations, her emotional overload as a single mom and university student—in addition to her disappointing affair with Tom—could have seemed overwhelming at times. Dr. Halleck felt that her sadness was beyond the normal and reached a level allowing the diagnosis of depression. The state's psychiatrist, Dr. Donald Morgan, had diagnosed Susan as manifesting an Adjustment Disorder with Mixed Emotional Features, including some depression.[7] But is a form of clinical depression enough to explain her reaction of killing her children? The following questions are important:

- How does depression affect a person's thoughts and behavior?

- How could depression be a "cause" of Susan's killing her sons?

- What is the difference between how a mentally healthy person responds to such circumstances, compared to a mentally ill person?

- How was Susan different than millions of other custodial single-parent moms throughout our country?

- Since most depressed single parents do not kill their children, how is Susan different?

- What is different between a criminal mind and a mentally-disturbed mind? Which is Susan? Or could she be both mentally disturbed and a criminal?

- What forms of mental disorder make it impossible for a person to recognize the difference between right and wrong?

As previously mentioned, there have been various studies reporting lifetime occurrences of Major Depressive Disorders to be between 10 percent to 25 percent for women. Therefore, a sizable proportion of females have depression but a rare minority ever kill their children. In recent years in the United States, there have been annual reports of between 1400 to 2000 parents who killed their child. But 13 million to 32 million American women suffer Major Depression (a diagnosis more severe that Susan's diagnosis) at some point in their lives.

In South Carolina, there are four possible pleas to the charge of murder:

- Guilty

- Guilty but Mentally Ill

- Not Guilty

- Not Guilty by Reason of Insanity

Susan's defense attorneys would have been hard-pressed to enter a plea of "not guilty" after Susan had already signed a confession in the presence of law enforcement officers. There was no advantage to pleading "guilty," because then there would be no jury trial and the judge would simply sentence her.

Instead of entering a plea, months before the trial they informed the judge that they would plead either "Not Guilty by Reason of Insanity," or "Guilty but Mentally Ill." The disadvantage of the latter plea is that the judge could sentence Susan to death, which sentence could be carried out once her mental illness was treated.

But having just any mental illness is not the same as the legal meaning of "insanity." That boils the key question for sentencing down to this:

- Was Susan insane at the time of the crime?

- Was Susan sane and evil to kill her sons and then lie about it?

- Or was she truly a "victim"?

According to her confession,

> When I was at John D. Long Lake, I had never felt so scared and unsure as I did then. I wanted to end my life so bad and was in my car ready to go down that ramp into the water, and I did go part way, but I stopped. I went again and stopped. I then got out of the car and stood by the car a nervous wreck.
>
> Why was I feeling this? Why was everything so bad in my life? I had no answers to these questions. I dropped to the lowest point when I allowed my children to go down that ramp into the water without me.

Pieced together from what Susan told various investigators, such as FBI agent Carol Allison, according to law enforcement testimony at Susan's trial, Susan hoped that she would not hear her sons cries for help and the car splashing into the lake. She put her hands over her ears and ran to the top of the boat ramp. According to Susan's written confession,

> I took off running and screaming, "Oh God! Oh God, NO! What have I done? Why did you let this happen? I wanted to turn around so bad and go back, but I knew it was too late.

Susan told agent Allison, "I can't understand why I didn't go in the lake." But the fact is, Susan did not run toward the car to get her boys out before the car sank.

The videotaped re-enactment of Susan's Mazda and another similar Mazda showed that the car took a full six minutes to gradually become submerged in the lake. In fact, it came to light in the courtroom testimony of Steve M. Derrick, Senior Investigator of the State Law Enforcement Division, that as the recovered car was dredged from the lake, it had all its doors closed, the doors unlocked, and all the windows closed. This is why it would have taken a full six minutes for the car to completely sink and for the interior to be completely filled with water.

It was not just Susan's momentary impulse to release the car with her boys into the lake. Her boys' deaths required Susan's repeated choice over those six minutes to refuse to run back to retrieve her helpless children from the car before it completely filled with water to vanish beneath the surface of the cold and murky lake water.

Then, no doubt, Susan experienced a keen conflict: She panicked over her murder of her own children, and this only increased her sense of loneliness and depression. In her confession, she wrote,

> I was an absolute mental case! I couldn't believe what I had done.
> . . . I am sorry for what has happened. . . . I don't think I will ever be able to forgive myself for what I have done.

Despite that these murders were not unique, and that thousands of children are reportedly murdered by a parent each year, the story of the drowning of Michael and Alex gripped the nation like no other comparable case. At first, the national news media carried the story of the alleged kidnapping of the handsome little boys from their seemingly safe, remote little rural town of Union, South Carolina on October 25, 1994. But after nine days of concerted searching, the news story took the unexpected and bizarre twist that the boys' own mother confessed to drowning them in her car at a nearby lake.

A "murdering mother" is a frustrating oxymoron that, in this case, demands much explaining: those two words—"murdering" and "mother"—just don't fit together. Killing one's own children is an imponderable treachery—indeed, the unthinkable crime. We expect every mother will instinctively care for and lovingly protect her dependent little ones. And yet the true story of the internationally publicized case of Susan Smith uncomfortably forces the public to come to terms with the admitted fact that Susan did indeed drown her two little sons by releasing her car into a lake.

- Why in the world did she do it?
- What was she thinking or feeling at the time of the crime?

- Was she psychotic—totally out of touch with reality?

- Did her own father's suicide twist her mind as she was growing up as a child herself?

- Did sexual abuse by her stepfather push her over the edge mentally?

- Was Susan actually mentally ill at the time of the crime so she could not tell the difference between right and wrong?

- Was she insane?

- Isn't anyone who kills his or her own children "insane" by definition?

- Can there be a valid excuse for this crime?

- Is she as much a victim as her sons?

- Why did she pose as a victim of a child kidnapper and then later confess to killing her own sons?

- Does Susan Smith really deserve the death penalty, a prison term, or psychiatric care?

These types of questions and issues can and will be found in millions of conversations across the U.S. and are at the forefront of the public's attention now, as they were during the months of Susan Smith's trial, and as they will be for some time to come.

Susan Smith's trial presented facts that will help the public gain a deeper understanding of the psychology of victims and the conditions for legal responsibility for one's behavior. The general public desires a better understanding of what went on in Susan's mind and heart that dark night in October 1994 when her boys were drowned.

According to the American common law followed in the State of South Carolina, a person is held legally responsible for his or her behavior, if, at the time,

- that person was capable of voluntarily performing the act (this is called *actus reus* in legal terms), and
- that person was capable of forming the intention to act (this is called *mens rea* in legal terms).[8]

If either *actus reus* or *mens rea* are significantly impaired by a mental defect, a mental illness, or other condition that the person cannot control, then that person can be excused from the normal legal consequences, such as punishment.

What mental disorders are considered as affecting *actus reus* (the person's voluntary control over their actions)? Here is one example: Suppose you had a house guest stay overnight in your home. Your guest has a history of suffering from a sleepwalking disorder when he sleeps at night. After he falls asleep in your guest bedroom, he unconsciously starts to sleepwalk, wandering in your house, and he happens to see some of your jewelry which he picks up and puts in his suitcase before getting back into bed. The next morning, he cordially thanks you for having him over and leaves, without knowing that your jewelry is in his suitcase. If the sleepwalking is not under your guest's voluntary, conscious control, his lawyer could defend him as having impaired *actus reus* if you were to take him to court for stealing your jewelry.

Some other disorders that can impair voluntary control are:

- postconcussion syndrome
- epilepsy

- anoxia (lack of oxygen to the brain)
- the dissociative disorder of psychogenic fugue, and
- the dissociative disorder of multiple personality.[9]

What are the types of mental disorders, which are considered as affecting *mens rea?*

Suppose, for example, that a woman with the paranoid type of schizophrenia develops a delusion that her young child is about to kill her. As a result, the woman physically assaults her child entirely without any provocation, continuing to beat the child until he dies. Courtroom testimony by a clinical psychologist or psychiatrist that the woman's assault on her child was triggered by a persecutory delusion would most likely result in a verdict of Not Guilty by Reason of Insanity (known in the legal and mental health professions as NGRI) or Guilty but Mentally Ill (GBMI).

Some other disorders, which are generally found in a court of law to interfere with the capability of forming the intention to act are:

- Other forms of psychoses
- Mental retardation, and
- Bipolar disorder (manic-depressive illness)

With Susan's mental disorder, would she have committed the act of sending her boys into the lake trapped in the car if a police officer were standing at the boat ramp observing her?

The answer to this question is one way to understand the legal test for "insanity" in that an "insane" person does not recognize right from wrong and would perform the crime even in the presence of a police officer. "Insanity" is a legal concept and not a diagnostic term of the mental health professions. An insanity defense is the attempt, on behalf of a criminal defendant, to be excused for misconduct on the basis of his or her mental condition at the time of the crime. The most widely used insanity defense standards are 1) the American Law Institute test and 2) the M'Naghten tests.

In the state of South Carolina, if a person accused of a crime is found to have a mental disease or defect that renders him or her unable to distinguish moral *or* legal right from moral or legal wrong, or if that mental disease or defect renders him or her unable to recognize the particular act charged as morally or legally wrong, that person would be found Not Guilty by Reason of Insanity.[10]

Another South Carolina statute[11] holds that the "inability to control one's acts is not a complete defense to criminal acts."[12] In such a case, the person's impairment contributing to a crime would result in a verdict of Guilty but Mentally Ill, which can result in either prison time or probation, depending upon the particular crime involved.[13] According to my distinguished colleague, Dr. Geoffrey McKee, the recent president of the American Academy of Forensic Psychology, ". . . mental illness in and of itself may not excuse a person from legal responsibility in either criminal or domestic matters."[14]

During the opening statements of Susan's trial, one of her defense attorneys, Judy Clarke, insisted, "We are not here to talk to you about any abuse excuse. We are not here to put on evidence of excusing responsibility because of bad circumstances in life or an abused life, because Susan Smith accepts responsibility for what happened."

Instead, Susan's defense attorneys outlined her emotional troubles, which they portrayed as pushing her to drown her two sons. They believed that showing her emotional problems would save her from the electric chair.[15]

Even though Susan Smith's defense attorneys hoped to influence the jury to view Susan Smith sympathetically in forming their verdict and sentence of her, they did not claim she was insane and did not prove that her mental illness caused her to kill the boys.[16]

6

The Hoax: Why Did Her "Victim Mentality" Get Out of Hand?

Shuddering with fear, Susan turned her back to the lake, put her hands over her ears so she could not hear her boys cry or the car splash, and jogged up the boat ramp, away from the stark horror of what she had just done at John D. Long Lake. It was all too clear and vivid in her mind.[1] *"Oh God! O God, No!" What have I done? Why did I let this happen? I sent my babies into the lake."*

Her heart pounded and her palms grew sweaty. All of a sudden, she wanted so badly to turn around and go back in time to reverse her actions. But the car had sunk beneath the surface, and she knew it was too late. Now, she could hardly believe what she had done. As the electrifying sensation of panic shot through her whole being, one thought predominated, *"I have to get out of here. I just have to get out of here."*

A confusing swirl of emotions flooded her consciousness with twinges of sharp panic, pounding anxiety, foreboding apprehension, piercing guilt, and a hauntingly lonely, dark depression. She desperately tried to comfort herself with the soothing thought, *"My babies are in heaven now, free of all pain. They will never, ever suffer again."* Such thinking was supposed to help her feel a relief for her boys and a freedom for herself from the trap of motherhood so she could focus her mind on all the new exciting possibilities for romantic living in the here and now. But somehow, she felt all the more weighted down. It was so confusing.

Running to the top of the ramp, her thoughts turned from her feelings of isolation to the jolting realization that she quickly needed to summon help for her story to work. Her only hope now for sympathy, especially from her recently lost lover, Tom Findlay, would be to cunningly pose as a tragic victim in dire need of help and massive emotional support.

Susan wrapped her arms around Tom's Auburn University sweat shirt she was wearing. She felt closer to Tom wearing his sweat shirt. By "hugging herself," she could imagine being comforted by Tom's affectionate embrace, once he learned of how her kids were "kidnapped" and taken from her. How she yearned for his embrace right now!

Strangely, his Auburn sweat shirt served as a glowing momentary comfort in this dark, lonely moment. Although Tom had acted painfully remote lately, she had reminded him that she would be a loyal friend, and that she would do *anything* for Tom—absolutely anything! *"If only he knew the depths of how devoted I am to him,"* she thought.

She determined not to consider, not even for a moment, any possibility of telling the truth now. There was too much at stake. She didn't want to waste the one opportunity she had—the opportunity that she had created for herself at John D. Long Lake. All possibilities for reconciliation with Tom would be absolutely destroyed by the truth. She chose not to let that happen.

Thus she made the cunningly evil choice against the truth and in favor of deception, and all for quite selfish reasons—for self-preservation and to draw the loving attention that a victim stance could bring to her. There was nothing remotely heroic in this. She had not courageously risked her life to rescue her children. Quite the opposite. She decided to do all she could to cover up the gruesome truth of what she had heartlessly done to her own little boys.

After running only a short distance, Susan noticed a light coming from someone's house—the opportunity she needed. "*Someone must be home,*" she thought. Panting, she broke into a rapid sprint down the road toward the house, while, at the same time, all along rehearsing an invented story to explain what happened to her car and to her little boys. She would be the passive, helpless victim, instead of her boys. Out of breath by now and shaking all over, she had to stop, bend over, and pause briefly just before continuing on to reach the front yard of the lighted house.

With an almost automatic determination to share her phony story as convincingly as possible, Susan knew she would need to act well, once again.

But now, she reminded herself again, "*Life will be free of all pain for Michael and Alex in heaven, and for the first time, my life will be free of pain, too, with a definite chance with Tom now.*" But her emotions were strongly ambivalent. For a few agonizing minutes, she vacillated between depressed suicidal thoughts of wanting to die right now to join Michael and Alex in heaven on the one hand, and her own self-preservation and self-centered desires to get on with her own life here on earth, on the other hand. These conflicting, strong desires collided with such force that she felt overwhelmed.

But there was an obstacle to committing suicide in her mind: Susan had very serious doubts that any person who commits suicide could actually go to heaven. For years, she had ruminated on the devastating possibility that her beloved father was suffering the torments of hell because he had chosen to kill himself.

In a strange way, now, she felt trapped by her own decision to kill little Michael and Alex. She felt overwhelmed with a sense of profound loss rather than the anticipated thrill of freedom from the number one obstacle to a permanent intimate relationship with Tom. Her feelings were getting all mixed up, and she suddenly felt so alone, so guilty, and increasingly despondent. Her tears flowed naturally and profusely, and her body still shook all over.

"I need to be with someone. *I've got to get into that house right now to call Mama,*" she thought. She convinced herself that she would have to play it up for all she was worth this time, and she cunningly realized that her voluminous tears would help her story fly.

Moaning out loud, Susan ran directly to the front door of Shirley and Rick McCloud's home a little after 9 p.m. on that Tuesday evening, October 25, 1994. She dramatically banged on their door with vigorous urgency, screaming, "Please help me! Please help me! Oooooohhh, pleeease help me now!"

This startled the McClouds, not only the screaming and loud banging, but also because any knock at the front door was so extremely rare at their home. All family members and everyone else who knew them always came to the side entrance instead. Shirley McCloud immediately dropped the *Union Daily Times* on the floor and dashed to the front door, with her husband Rick close behind.

Shirley made sure the chain was secure and unlocked the door a crack to see who it was. She saw Susan standing in the hazy light on the porch, crying hysterically. Shirley quickly unfastened the chain and swung the door open wide.

Susan immediately pleaded, "Please help me! Please help me, he's got my kids in my car!" The sheer terror in Susan's voice alarmed Shirley. She instinctively wrapped her arm around Susan's shoulders and gently guided her into the house, as Susan leaned up against her.

Shirley escorted Susan to a love seat, and calmly tried to prompt Susan to explain her problem. In the meantime, Rick McCloud shouted to his son, "Rick Junior, call 911 right now!"

Susan seemed barely able to talk, but she managed to blurt out, "A black man has got my kids and my car." Rick Junior was listening and echoed Susan's complaints to the emergency dispatcher. He added a description of Susan's reactions, "ma'am, she's real hysterical and . . . I need . . . the law down here." Calling the Union County deputy sheriffs, the dispatcher logged the call at 9:12 p.m.[2]

As soon as the phone was put down, Rick grabbed the keys to their 1993 Pontiac Bonneville and yelled for Rick Junior to dash out with him to search for Susan's car and her kidnapped kids.

Shirley tried to get the whole story from Susan by kneeling in front of her and taking her face in her hands. Shirley felt Susan's moist, clammy skin and recognized her short rapid gasps for air. "Tell me, now, from the beginning, what happened."[3]

Susan's tears flowed in a fresh gush, but she got out the words, "While I was stopped at the red light back there at Monarch, a black man jumped into my car and ordered me to drive on. When I asked him, 'Why are you doing this to me?' he yelled, 'Shut up and just drive.' Then I remember passing the sign."

"What sign? Shirley gently asked.

"That John Long sign," Susan explained as she pointed back over her shoulder. This is the sign only a couple hundred yards from the McCloud's house.

"Then he said, 'Stop here,' right in the middle of the road, and told me to get out. So I asked, 'Please give me my kids,' but he says, 'Shut up. Don't worry lady, I won't hurt your kids.' I blurted out, 'Why can't I take my kids?' But he said, 'I don't have time,' and he kept trying to push me out of the car.

"I dropped to the ground, and he took off. Then I got up and started to run when I saw the lights at your house."

After asking to use the bathroom, Susan told Shirley, "I need to call my mama." Shirley quickly dialed the phone number as Susan called it out. Susan's oldest brother Michael answered, but explained that Susan's mother, Linda, had just left. Susan relayed a message through Shirley to ask Michael to try to find her mother, and Shirley conveyed Susan's story to Michael.

Then Susan asked to call her stepfather, Bev Russell, but her hands were trembling too much to press the buttons. Shirley graciously assisted in dialing. Shirley recognized Bev's name, knowing his TV and appliance store, as most anyone would in Union. Reaching Mr. Russell, Shirley told him what Susan told her about the children and handed the phone to Susan who tearfully repeated her carjacking/kidnapping story.

Then, after Bev promised to come right over, Susan wanted to call David at Winn-Dixie. Susan jabbered, cried, and wailed hysterically over the phone so David could barely comprehend what was going on. Shirley urgently tried to explain the situation to David, but by then, she too was overcome with so much emotion that she could not be much more coherent. But David promised he'd race over as fast as he could.[4]

Dark apprehension and a confusing swirl of emotions

flooded David's heart, "I thought I was going to go out of my mind as I drove out there," he said. "I'd never experienced that kind of fear. I didn't know how to react."[5]

Sheriff Howard Wells of Union County promptly arrived as did some of his deputies. As Sheriff Wells walked into the McCloud's living room, his detective mind noted a number of small details. Susan was wearing a gray sweat shirt with orange writing that spelled "Auburn." Her face was puffy and red, and her face rested in her hands. Susan described the abductor as wearing a plaid jacket with red, blue, and some white. She described his gun as "dark." She reported that three-year-old Michael was wearing a white jogging suit. Fourteen-month-old Alex was wearing a red and white striped outfit. The children were in her burgundy 1990 Mazda Protégé, with a gash in its right front bumper. But Susan could not recall her tag number.

And within minutes of their arrival, police station computer terminals all over the United States contained the urgent message to be on the lookout for a black man driving a burgundy Mazda Protégé with two white preschooler boys in the back seat.[6]

Posing as a deeply grieving victim of a sinister armed Afro-American kidnapper, Susan was already drawing the affectionate nurturing from everyone around her. She sucked it all in like a powerfully insatiable vacuum cleaner. Soon, the McCloud residence was filled with people who hugged her and tried to comfort her. Susan's long-time friend, Donna Garner, Donna's boyfriend, Mitchell Sinclair, Donna's parents, Walt and Barb, and Susan's mother, Linda, and stepfather, Bev, came.

Already, a SLED helicopter with a heat sensor was patrolling the dense forest nearby, picking up any signs of life or car by detecting heat radiating from the object. But they later reported detecting only wildlife. Divers were dispatched to search John D. Long Lake nearby, but they turned up nothing.

By midnight with nothing yet solved, the sheriff asked that Susan suggest another meeting place so the McClouds could get their rest that night. Susan immediately volunteered her mother's home. Susan, David, family and friends migrated over to the Russell home in Mount Vernon Estates, a subdivision of expensive homes west of town.

Susan rode with David in his Honda, but as he headed toward the Russell home on Heathwood Road, Susan insisted, "I want to go to Toney Road." She said she needed to get her contact lenses and a few other things from their little brick home. David agreed. But with his mind still focused on Michael and Alex, he kept firing questions about their abduction, hoping to jog her memory with some details that might solve the case.

Then, after an uncomfortable silence in the car, Susan calmly made the statement that struck David as entirely strange: "Listen, Tom Findlay might come and see me. If he comes down, you can't get mad or anything. I don't want you two to get into a fight."

David simply could not believe his ears. Here they were in a crisis with their sons missing, and Susan is telling him that she's so concerned that he not get upset if her boyfriend comes to visit.

Thus began the famous and highly expensive nine day national search for Michael and Alex Smith. Susan was the absolute center of attention for her family, for Union, and for the watching world. David stayed right beside her to console her and to help her remember anything more about the alleged abductors of their children.

In the past, Susan had mastered the habit of evading responsibility for her own actions by blaming others for victimizing her. Except this time, she was doing it on a much grander scale. The deception was perfectly twisted: The merciless perpetrator of cold-blooded murder posed as the helpless victim of kidnapping.

Tom Findlay did make a very brief telephone call to Susan the next day after he heard the news of the kidnapping. Susan Smith's friend, Susan Brown, had called Tom Findlay on his car phone while he was driving to Charlotte, North Carolina. She informed him of the news of the kidnapping of the Smith children, and gave Tom the Russell home phone number where the Smiths were staying.

Then Tom made a brief call to Susan to express his sympathies about her children. But the first thing Susan said to Tom was that she was sorry for what she had said to him, shifting the whole topic of the conversation to their relationship.[7] Tom replied, "Don't worry about it. Let's concentrate on your kids."[8]

Friends sensitively and generously nurtured Susan's emotions and provided for her needs. And the physical comfort of hugs were everywhere for Susan. It was so comforting to always have someone with her. She was never alone now. So many people came to visit and stay with her while she awaited news of her children.

Except, where was Tom? When her friend and co-worker at Conso Products, Susan Brown, came to visit her, Susan Smith walked outdoors with her and asked her to tell Tom she wanted him to come visit her.[9] But Tom wasn't showing up, as Susan had expected. Tom didn't take her bait.

On Wednesday, October 26, 1994—one day after the alleged kidnapping—newspaper reporter Gary Henderson of the nearby Spartanburg *Herald-Journal* landed an exclusive interview with Susan. She retold her story about the kidnapper to him, but he was frankly surprised that Susan never broke down crying.[10] Others immediately wondered, "How could she let him drive away with them in the car and not put up a fight?"[11]

Henderson's photographer for the story, Mike Bonner, couldn't believe Susan's story from the beginning. It just made no sense at all to him. Chatting with Bonner, even Henderson wondered out loud, "Why would a black man on the run want two screaming children in the back seat of the car?"[12] And white children at that. Wouldn't that be awfully suspicious?

Susan would not look reporters in the eye. But David did look at them very directly. His grief-filled red eyes and distraught expressions touched the most hardened reporters. As David held Susan's hand, she spoke to the reporters.

"If they are lying somewhere dead, I want them home. Oh, God, I can't bear to think of that,"[13] Susan said to the reporters while looking at the floor.

David openly revealed, "Every time the phone rings, I cringe because I don't know what news we'll hear. I still have a lot of hope they are out there somewhere okay. I could not go on if I lose hope. This all seems unbelievable."[13]

Quickly, the local TV, radio, and newspaper reporters were joined by all the national networks, and some correspondents from European and Australian media as well. Satellite trucks, cameras, and reporters swarmed in front of the Russell residence where David and Susan were staying. As the kidnapping story gained national press coverage, millions weeped over the tragedy. Thrust onto center stage of media attention, Susan became a central actress for evening TV news, radio reports, and front page newspaper stories.

Because of her professional experience in regularly dealing with the media, Margaret Gregory tried to help

David and Susan Smith cope with the onslaught of the media during Susan's nine-day kidnapping hoax. Margaret (who is married to Susan Smith's cousin) works in the media department of the Richland County Sheriff's Department. Because Susan was so reluctant to face the scrutiny of the press, Margaret denied most requests for media interviews and conversations with others. Even Marc Klaas, the founder of the Marc Klaas Foundation for Children, which assists the parents of missing children, was turned away because of Susan's reluctance.

Time was slipping away. Each day, law enforcement officials increasingly doubted her story. From the beginning little clues here and there began to raise doubts in some minds, and her "perfect" little reconstruction of reality began to gradually unravel at the edges.

Early in his investigation, the sheriff's deputies interrogated both David and Susan.

On Wednesday, October 26, David informed them that Susan was seeing other men. They wanted details. Names. For how long? David told them that Tom Findlay seemed to be the most recent of Susan's boyfriends, but that they had just broken off the relationship. But David was frustrated by all this attention directed to Susan. He didn't want law enforcement officers to divert time and attention from the search for his boys.[14] The officers tried to calm David by telling him that they just wanted to get the inconsistencies of the case straightened out.

At 4:20 a.m. on October 26, the Union Sheriff's office called David A. Caldwell, Director of Forensic Sciences Laboratory for the State Law Enforcement Division, to come from Columbia to Union to interview Susan Smith. That same day around noon, he interviewed Susan in the sheriff's offices.

Agent Caldwell asked Susan to relate the details of the

day of October 25, starting when she woke up until 911 was called.[15] Among many other things, Susan said, "When I got home from work, I called my mother to see if I could come over, but she had other plans. So I made pizza for the kids. But the kids were fussy. At 7:30 p.m., Michael said he wanted to go to Wal-Mart.

"Michael suggested Wal-Mart?" Agent Caldwell asked.

"Well, no, I suggested it," Susan replied. And she said they went and stayed there until 8:40 p.m. Then she said she drove to Foster Park, but didn't get out. Then she claimed that she returned to the Wal-Mart parking lot to make use of the light there because Alex had dropped his bottle on the floor. "Then Michael said he wanted to see Mitch," Susan continued.

"Michael suggested visiting Mitch?" the agent asked.

"Well, no, not actually. I suggested it," Susan replied.

Then on the way to Mitch's, Susan explained how she stopped at a red light at the intersection of Monarch, but saw no other cars there. Then the black man jumped into her car with a gun. She related her whole story.

Agent Caldwell asked her, "Did he cuss?"

"No," replied Susan with certainty.

"Did he have bad B.O.?"

"No."

"Did he seem crazy?"

"No, but he seemed real nervous. You could hear it in his voice when he said, 'Drive, drive,' " Susan said.

Then Agent Caldwell told Susan, "We have to rule out every possibility. We have information that you have a boyfriend, Tom Findley, and that he is not interested in pursuing a relationship with you because of your children. Did this fact play any role or have any bearing on the disappearance of your children?"

Susan smiled. "No man would make me hurt my children. They were my life."[16] Susan curiously answered in

the past tense (as though the children no longer were living). At the trial, Agent Caldwell noted that from time to
time in his interview with Susan, she would sob, but tears
would not always accompany her apparent crying. "When
there were tears shed, she would look up, and hold her
tearful cheek toward me"[17]

When he interviewed her on October 28, Susan would
not look him in the eye when he talked to her. Instead, she
would turn and face the corners of the 8x10 foot room and
speak her answers to the walls. Furthermore, when Agent
Caldwell first asked Susan to take her first polygraph test,
she looked at him and asked, "What if I fail?" These unusual
responses made him suspicious of Susan's story.

Susan had told investigators that she had taken her
boys to Wal-Mart on the previous evening and then
headed for Mitch Sinclair's place. Then when stopped at
the red light at Monarch, the abductor jumped into the
car. She reported seeing no other car.

But no one reported seeing Susan and her boys at Wal-
Mart that evening, and Mitch had not expected her, and
he was not home at that time. And the light at Monarch is
always green unless triggered by cross traffic which acti-
vates the red light, so she should have seen another car
passing while stopped at a red light at that intersection.
But David dismissed these discrepancies as a product of an
emotionally distraught mother.[18]

Furthermore, the forensic artist, Roy Paschal, who
made the police sketch from Susan's description, knew
that she had just directed him to draw an imaginary suspect. Susan had described a black male, medium build,
with plaid coat and a toboggan hat. As all professional
forensic artists, Mr. Paschal was trained to look for false
allegations when informants describe a suspect.

In Susan's case, she began extremely vague in her description of the kidnapper, and then she got very minutely

specific as to details that belonged in the drawing. "That was highly unusual," testified Mr. Pascal later in Susan's murder trial.

Further, the police artist's suspicions were raised at the end of the session when he asked her if she wanted to say anything else. Susan brightened and asserted, "I feel like when the sun comes up, they'll find my children." It sounded rehearsed the way she said it.

When he asked her how she liked the drawing, she said, "It looks just like him." She told the artist, "I like the way you draw. I'll call around Christmas to ask you to do a drawing of my child . . . (she stopped in the middle of the word "children," and did not finish that sentence).

Then the artist asked how her husband was doing, and Susan said, "We're separated, expecting a divorce."

The artist asked, "Do you have a boyfriend?"

"No," Susan replied.

"I mean, it's not uncommon for separated people to have a boyfriend," the artist offered, fearing he had offended her.

"Yeah, I do have a boyfriend. Here's a sweat shirt of his from Auburn University," Susan said with a brightened mood as she held up the sweat shirt.

Later on October 26 when Susan was interviewed again by Agent Caldwell of SLED, he asked her, "Why haven't you been completely honest with the police?"

Susan replied in a frustrated, distraught manner, "I admit I never went to Wal-Mart the two times to visit and later to get light to find the baby bottle."

"Why," asked Agent Caldwell, "did you say it, then?"

"There's something I'm embarrassed about. If I just said I just drove around, you'd think I sounded dumb, so I made up the Wal-Mart thing."[19]

On a third occasion on the same day, Agent Caldwell again interviewed Susan in Deputy Gregory's office. This time he confronted her strongly on her inconsistencies. "Why didn't you tell us the truth about the phone calls and about Wal-Mart? You can see why we're so suspicious of you."

"Yes, Susan replied. "We were just driving around, and the kids were singing."

At that, Agent Caldwell confronted Susan directly. "You said before that your kids were fussy and your husband told us that he heard them being fussy when he called you on the phone just before you left the house. They were fussy. IS THAT WHY YOU KILLED THEM?"

At that comment, Susan slammed her fist on the table. "You son of a b----. How can you think that! I want to leave."

As Susan quickly walked out into the hall, she shouted, "I can't believe that you think *I* did it!"

Then on Thursday, October 27, Susan was asked to take a polygraph test by an FBI agent, David Allen Espie, III, in the jury room of the Union County courthouse, a session which began around 11:40 a.m. and lasted much of the afternoon. Agent Espie had Susan read and sign a form advising her of her Miranda rights—her right to remain silent, her right to an attorney, her right to stop talking or to leave at any time once they begin. Susan signed that statement and also a "Waiver of Rights," indicating her willingness to make the statement and that no promises or threats had been made to her.

Susan was not under arrest at the time. She wasn't very specific about the events on the night of October 25, Once again, she said that she decided to go to Wal-Mart, leaving home at 8 p.m. and arriving at 8:10 p.m. She claimed she had been there until 8:35 or 8:40 p.m. "She was very specific as to what they did. They were looking for toys for Christmas. She was specific about how happy Michael was. She mentioned that they spent time looking at the fish tank area. Then she said she departed Wal-Mart without making a purchase."[20]

Again, Susan said she asked Michael if he wanted to go to Mitch's house. Michael was excited to go. Then she claimed that she stopped at the red light at Monarch, and suddenly a black man came into the car with a gun.

Throughout this interview, Susan seemed to be taken aback by the presence of the FBI in this case. She expressed that she was not aware that the case would go beyond the Union County Sheriff's office. In this interview, Agent Espie described Susan as making "fake sounds of crying with no tears in her eyes."[21] He also said that she would make crying sounds at inappropriate times, appearing to avoid answering certain questions. "The last sixty minutes of the interview she made only one comment."[22]

Susan replied, "How could you think I could harm or abuse the children?"[23] Then she made sounds of crying but had no tears again. Agent Espie offered Susan tissues, but there was no need for the tissues.[24] At the end of the session, Susan cried on David's shoulder, complaining that they suspected her of doing something with the children and that they did not believe her story.

At a 5 p.m. press conference on Friday, October 28, Sheriff Wells announced that he had not ruled out any suspects, including the parents. He further stated that investigators had discovered some discrepancies in Susan's statements, but he would not specify what they were. [25] In the meantime, thousands of telephone calls and leads poured into the sheriff's office, which pursued the search aspect of the investigation in the effort to locate Michael and Alex. But all along, the parallel investigation was to "crack their mother's lie into smithereens."[26]

Now that it was public that law enforcement officials doubted Susan's story, would Tom Findlay hear of it? Would this reduce chances that he would come visit Susan and embrace her? Would this jeopardize Susan's prospects for a romance with him after all?

Tom still had not visited Susan since the disappearance of her boys. Susan had Margaret fending off all the reporters and others she did not want to see. But the one person Susan wanted to come by—Tom—never came.

On the following Wednesday, November 2, Margaret convinced the Smiths to appear for a news conference on the steps of the Union County Courthouse. This was in hopes of keeping Michael and Alex in the news to aid their recovery. It was Margaret who also arranged for interviews before all three major TV networks on Thursday, November 3rd, just several hours before Susan confessed.

Interviews of David and Susan were taped for the morning shows of NBC and CBS, and the couple appeared live on ABC. By this time, Susan was defending herself against the widespread speculation that her story was false.

"I did not have anything to do with the abduction of my children," Susan insisted on *CBS This Morning*. "I don't think that any parent could love their children more than I do, and I would never even think about doing anything that would harm them," Susan continued in that interview. "It's really painful to have the finger pointed at you when it's your children. Whoever did this is a sick and emotionally unstable person," Susan contended.

Although David was legally separated from Susan at the time, when he was directly asked whether he believed his wife, he replied curtly, "Yes. I believe my wife totally."[27]

Susan's storytelling, beginning on the night of October 25, 1994, was not an isolated event in her life—as though somehow detached from all her past history. Those who live and speak such huge lies are often trapped by their false communications, causing them to dig ever deeper into deceit and deception to keep covering their tracks from past evil and past falsehoods they have perpetrated. But often, especially when the life and death stakes are high, a lifestyle of deception collapses into shambles after too many details just don't add up. It happened that way for Susan, and the balloon of her "victim stance" instantly exploded.

7

The Confession: Did She Abandon the "Victim Mentality" or Merely Continue it in a New Way?

"I feel mentally abused at home. David doesn't like me to go out. Once David even drug me out of bed onto the porch," Susan complained, as she explained her marriage, separations, and her recent filing for divorce on grounds of adultery. SLED Agent, James Logan (South Carolina State Law Enforcement Division), also got Susan to speak of her relationship with Tom Findlay.

Logan also listened to Susan talk of failure. "I've let people down. I feel that I've let everybody down."[1] This was part of his interrogation plan, and it was succeeding like clockwork.

Susan related well to James Logan because of his warm southern gentlemanly manner, which he had picked up living in the South for so many years. But it was more than southern pleasantries that he was trying to communicate. He had a plan.

Logan is a highly-skilled, seasoned criminal investigator with thirty-five years of law enforcement experience. After serving in the military, he joined the FBI in 1961, where he served for twenty-seven years. Included in his work was the investigation of the assassination of President John F. Kennedy. In more recent years, he has served as an agent for the South Carolina State Law Enforcement Division.

Between 10 and 10:30 a.m. on Saturday morning, October 29, 1994, Logan received a phone call at home from Major Christopher asking him to come to Union. Major Christopher informed Agent Logan that Susan Smith had walked out on some interviews by officers. By 2 p.m. the same day, Logan interviewed Susan for the first time. He also interviewed her on the following Sunday, Tuesday, and Wednesday, and spoke with her by phone on that Monday.[2]

Logan used a different approach than the other investigators who had worked with Susan. With the goal of keeping Susan talking, he tried to convey compassion and empathy, hoping to gain her confidence.[3]

That's why, in addition to getting Susan's story of the alleged carjacking and kidnapping of her children, Logan had Susan talking about her marriage and other relationships with men.

But by Wednesday, November 2nd—the 8th day since the alleged carjacking and disappearance of the children—the burgundy Mazda Protégé still had not been recovered, and there was no trace of her boys. Based upon Susan's interview answers in twenty-four hours of his personal questioning, and based on his decades of criminal investigative experience, Logan concluded that Susan was not telling the total truth.[4] Gently, he began to explore with her the puzzle of the red light at Monarch.

Logan drove to that intersection earlier to verify that the light would not be red at Monarch unless another car was crossing the intersection. He and the other law enforcement investigators regularly consulted with the FBI behavioral experts at Quantico, Virginia, on Susan's case. Those criminal experts predicted that if Susan were pressed about the impossibility of her story of seeing a red light at Monarch with no other cars crossing, that she would say, "Oh, of course. All along I've been thinking it was at Monarch, but instead it was the next intersection at Carlisle!" The experts were advised to be prepared for that response.

When Logan expressed the difficulty he had in trying to understand this seeming inconsistency in her story, Susan responded exactly as predicted, and claimed she really stopped at Carlisle. So Logan graciously thanked her for thinking this through with him, and he asked her to go home and write out a new revised description of the events of the evening of October 25.

By this time, Susan had already failed three polygraph "lie detector" tests. Several investigators had already directly accused her of lying, with one of them going so far as to bluntly accuse her of murdering her children. Logan told Sheriff Wells, "I feel we're close to Susan telling us something."[5]

Logan and Wells planned that the next day, Logan would get Susan's new statement, then have her talk with Wells. Their assumption, based upon the behavioral experts of the FBI, was that Susan would be more likely to confess to Wells. They also decided that Logan should not directly confront Susan and risk that she might stop talking to him. They needed Logan's continued interviewing of Susan in case she would not confess that next day, as they hoped.

On Thursday, November 3rd, Susan brought in her newly revised statement. But it said the same thing she had reported previously, with only the name "Monarch" changed to "Carlisle." Logan asked, "Anything else?" Getting nothing, Logan then had the sheriff talk to Susan.

Susan was getting close to revealing more of the truth. Why? Susan was worn down by the past eight days of intensive and lengthy interrogations. She had been facing increasingly skeptical and hostile news reporters, pressuring her for an explanation for the sheriff's report of unspecified "inconsistencies" in her story. She experienced some depression under this stress. And Sheriff Wells was a man she respected.[6]

Sheriff Wells took Susan to a stark room in the Family Center of the First Baptist Church, which is located just down the street from the Union County Courthouse. The sheriff and Susan sat kneecap to kneecap, facing one another, and they began to talk at 1:40 p.m.

"I know your story about the black carjacker is a lie. Here's why. You couldn't have stopped at Monarch at a red light if there were no other cars at the intersection. So you just now revised your story to say the carjacker jumped into your car at Carlisle instead of Monarch. But we know your back-up story is wrong, too, because that night I had my investigators at the Carlisle intersection working on an undercover drug case, and they reported to me that your car did not stop at that intersection either. My undercover officers would have seen the supposed black carjacker enter your car there. I'm going to have to tell this to the media in order to quell the rising tensions your accusation has caused among blacks here in Union."

Then Sheriff Wells looked Susan directly in the eyes, "This did not happen as you said."

Susan watched him closely. Then she pleadingly asked, "Sheriff, will you pray with me?"

Sheriff Wells, a devout Christian man, put his hands on Susan's hands and prayed. Among other things, during his prayer he said, "Lord, we know that all things will be revealed to us in time." Closing the prayer, he looked up at Susan and plainly said, "Susan, it is time."[7]

Susan dropped her head to her hands and blurted out, "I am so ashamed, I am so ashamed. I want your gun so I can kill myself."

"Why would you want to do that?" asked Wells.

"You don't understand, my children are not all right," Susan replied.

Then Susan fell to the floor, doubled over, heaving with emotion, sobbing deeply and uncontrollably. It was then 1:55 p.m. Trembling with emotion, Susan looked directly at Wells. He handed her a handkerchief to help her compose herself. Then she broke, and began to speek freely and openly about what had transpired on the evening of October 25.

Susan described loneliness, isolation, failure, and what a mess her life had become. She felt she could not be a good mother. "I didn't understand why everything bad was happening to me. I never felt so alone. I can't do anything right."

She wanted to die. But she didn't want her children not to have a mother. She could not understand how things went so badly in her life. Susan rocked in her chair, weeping.

"I wanted to go back, but I knew it was too late. The car was in the lake. But I believe that it didn't go into the water, but the Lord lifted the car away."[8] Inconsistently, Susan later told another officer, "I ran from the shore covering my ears so I couldn't hear the sounds of my Mazda slipping under the surface with my two boys strapped inside."

"I still don't understand how it happened the way it did," Susan wailed, with tears running down her face, dripping off her chin. "How could I have done this?"

Wells had been talking with Susan one-on-one. He then left the room, and Susan fell between two chairs weeping. Other investigators entered the room to obtain a written confession, including a veteran FBI agent, Carol Allison. Susan's emotions came in waves, and she collapsed in agent Allison's lap at one point.[9]

"I fear that my family will never forgive me. Do you think God could forgive me?" Susan implored agent Allison.

"Yes, and in time we will understand," replied Allison. "And your confession will be a gift to your grieving family. Maybe by understanding your experience, another family might be spared your pain."[10]

Susan seemed to have a problem with catching her breath, so much so that officers feared she might pass out from hyperventilating. She continued trembling, and would remove her glasses and put them back on.

"Susan, did you see which direction the car went into the water? The divers have been unable to find it in two recent searches of John B. Long lake," agent Allison inquired.

"No, I didn't see. I just ran. In fact, I covered my ears so I wouldn't hear anything and just ran," Susan insisted.

Within six hours of Susan's pleas for the return of her children from a kidnapper, broadcast nationally over the major television networks , she had confessed to killing her own children. On November 3, 1994, Susan wrote:

> When I left my home on Tuesday, October 25, I was very emotionally distraught. I didn't want to live anymore! I felt like things could never get any worse. When I left home, I was going to ride around a little while and then go to my mom's. As I rode and rode and rode, I felt even more anxiety coming upon me about not wanting to live. I felt I couldn't

be a good mom anymore but I didn't want my children to grow up without a mom. I felt I had to end our lives to protect us all from any grief or harm. I had never felt so lonely and so sad in my entire life. I was in love with someone very much, but he didn't love me, and never would. I had a very difficult time accepting that. But I had hurt him very much and I could see why he could never love me. When I was @ John D. Long Lake, [crossed out words here] I had never felt so scared and unsure as I did then. I wanted to end my life so bad and was in my car ready to go down that ramp into the water and I did go part way, but I stopped. I went again and stopped. I then got out of the car and stood by the car a nervous wreck. Why was I feeling this way? Why was everything so bad in my life? I had no answers to these questions. I dropped to the lowest when I allowed my children to go down that ramp into the water without me. I took off running and screaming "Oh God! O God, No!" What have I done? Why did you let this happen? I wanted to turn around so bad and go back, but I knew I was too late. I was an absolute mental case! I couldn't believe what I had done. I love my children w/ all my [drawn heart-shaped design]. That will never change. I have prayed to them for forgiveness and hope that they will find it in their [drawn heart-shaped design] to forgive me. I never meant to hurt them!! I am <u>sorry</u> for what has happened and I know that I need some help. I don't think I will ever be able to forgive myself for what I have done. My children, Michael and Alex, are with our Heavenly Father now and I know that they will never be hurt again. As a mom, that means more than words could ever say.

I knew from day one, the truth would prevail, but I was so scared I didn't know what to do. It was very tough emotionally to sit and watch my family hurt as they did. It was time to bring a peace of mind to everyone, including myself. My children deserve to have the best and now they will. I broke down on Thursday, November 3 and told Sheriff Howard Wells the truth. It wasn't easy, but after the truth was out, I felt like the world was lifted off my shoulders. I know now that it is going to be a tough and long road ahead of me. At this very moment, I don't feel I will be able to handle what's coming, but I have prayed to God that he give me the strength to survive each day and to face those times and situations in my life that will be extremely painful. I have put my total faith in God and He will take care of me.

Susan V. Smith

11/3/94

5:05 p.m.

Swiftly, after receiving Susan's confession, Sheriff Howard Wells put into motion a team of divers from the South Carolina Department of Natural Resources and SLED agents to secure and search John D. Long Lake for the car containing the bodies of Michael and Alex Smith.

Corporal Curtis Jackson was among the first divers to arrive at the scene. With guidance from his colleague, Mike Gault, the two of them entered a johnboat and paddled out onto the murky cold water of the lake. Jackson lowered himself out of the boat and dove down under the water. His first dive proved fruitless. Gault told Jackson more of the details learned from Susan Smith, and Jackson dove in again, this time locating the underside of the upside-down car within six minutes. But his light failed making it impossible to detect if the boys' bodies were in the car.

By then, higher ranking and more experienced divers, Sergeants Steve Morrow and Francis Mitchum, had arrived and suited up. Armed with more sophisticated diving lights, they quickly swam to the spot and dove for the car which was in approximately eighteen feet of water. The visibility was only twelve inches.

At first, they observed that all the windows were rolled up and all the doors were closed. Then the divers made a slow search around the burgundy Mazda Protégé. Then diver Steve Morrow saw something he'll never forget: "I saw a small hand against the window glass," he reported on the witness stand later.

"We had to be down on the bottom [of the lake] to see inside [the car]. . . . they were in car seats and hanging upside down. I was able to determine one occupant on either side of the vehicle. . . . [then] we proceeded back to shore and we related what we found to Sheriff Wells."

Shaken deeply by what they had seen, as the men came up out of the water, they were both crying.

After receiving all the confirmation he needed, Sheriff Wells raced from the lakeside to an awaiting SLED helicopter, which immediately lifted off to take him directly south to the home of Beverly and Linda Russell where David Smith was still staying. Landing on the front lawn of young neighbors two houses away, the helicopter door flew open, and Sheriff Wells raced to the Russell home where the family had already heard the unconfirmed Associated Press report that Susan had confessed to killing the children. The confirmation by Sheriff Wells, with his report of finding the boys' bodies in the lake, devastated their twenty-four-year-old father, David Smith. To the news that his precious sons were murdered, David screamed out in anguish and ran wildly around in total misery.

"My whole life had just been ripped from its frame. I was shell-shocked and grieving, and missing my boys so much."[11]

"Everything I'd planned—teaching them to play ball, taking them fishing, teaching them to ride a bike, watching them go to school that first day, watching them grow up—all that has been ripped from me, and I don't know what I'm supposed to do about it."[12]

As David recounted his reactions to the court in Susan's double murder trial, the twelve jurors literally sat on the edges of their chairs as the tearful, heartbroken father found it difficult to speak. At least three of the jurors cried with him.[13]

Tragically, according to a study by the United States Department of Justice, 88 percent of children who are killed are murdered by their parents. That is why parents are routinely investigated by law enforcement agencies in any report that their child is missing. Mothers are found to be the murderer in 55 percent of cases where a parent killed a child. Forty-eight percent of parents who kill their children were drinking alcohol prior to the crime. Only 14 percent of the parent murderers had a history of mental illness prior to the crime, as Susan Smith did.[14]

Sixty-four percent of the children murdered by a mother are sons and 36 percent are daughters. But there's not much difference in the gender of the children killed by fathers—52 percent are daughters and 48 percent are sons.

There continues to be a tragic "ripple effect" relating to the murders. David Smith was perhaps the first to experience permanent feelings of grief. "I emotionally, mentally shut down. The world stopped for me," is how David put it while answering a question on a nationally televised interview program.

When asked, "When did you face it?" David answered, "I'm still trying. Susan has changed my life for the rest of my life. She destroyed a lot of feelings I'll never have again. She robbed my time with the kids." David described the funeral for his boys as "a day I'll never forget because it's the day I had to bury my two sons. It brought such a deep grief I never knew existed."

On July 24, 1995, Margaret Gregory testified in the penalty phase of Susan's trial that she felt betrayed when Susan confessed to killing her boys.[15]

Customers at Wal-Mart viewed Sheriff Wells on TV announcing Susan's arrest for double murder. Twenty-seven-year-old assistant manager, Mark Ericksen recalls, "I remember that night. People were crying, cussing. A woman up at the service desk fell to her knees and said, 'Oh, my God!' "[16]

A strong hatred was directed toward Susan after she confessed to killing her little boys and perpetrating a hoax upon her community. Her own children were betrayed. Sons were stolen from David. And she betrayed her own community with the kidnapping hoax, accepting their sacrificial efforts to search for the boys, day after day.

Grandparents, aunts and uncles on both sides of the family lost their grandsons or nephews. This one act on one day totally destroyed any vestiges of Susan's marriage to David. It also guaranteed that Susan will be involuntarily institutionalized for many years, separated herself from her family.

The ripple effect includes financial and emotional costs

for many. Susan's lie cost the taxpayers approximately two million dollars for the extensive search for her boys who were presumed kidnapped. Untold emotional pain has been inflicted on those close to the boys in Union as well as on distant observers following the news around the world.

The defense psychiatrist, Dr. Seymour Halleck, proposed this theory: He emphasized that Susan had "intermittent depressive disorder," in which she only gets depressed when alone. And he clearly testified that when Susan becomes suicidal, it is when she is depressed. He also contended that Michael and Alex were the only source of unconditional love for Susan.

Something does not add up here.

If Susan were only suicidal when depressed, and only depressed when alone, she was not deeply depressed when with Michael and Alex, the only ones who gave her "unconditional love." Susan could not have been suicidal when her boys were with her. Therefore, what happened the night of October 25 could not have been a botched suicide. A media interview of five of the jurors in the Smith case revealed that the jury did not judge the trial evidence as backing the defense claim that the killing of the boys was a "botched suicide."

With her confession, Susan abandoned her child kidnapping victim role and assumed a different kind of victim role, aided and abetted by her defense attorneys. But her family recovered from the initial shock of her confession only to ask if they were to blame by missing earlier warning signs.

It would be expected that those closest to Susan might ask themselves, "Why didn't I see what she was like?" After the fact, it would be easy to ask oneself, "Were there some warning signs that she might harm the boys?" "Could I have done something differently that might have prevented this tragedy?"

Unfortunately, predicting this form of violence in a person with no prior history of murder is extremely difficult. After the fact, it is easy to imagine situations that could have been warning signs, but that is pure hindsight.

Susan's family needed to escape the uncomfortable guilt felt by Susan's blame-shifting to her mental illness. And they desperately wanted to save her from the death penalty, which they saw as heaping another loss upon two losses already. Bev Russell hired a leading death penalty defense lawyer, David Bruck, to defend Susan. Her mother Linda released a copy of one of Susan's letters from prison, depicting her sadness at not having some object, such as a baby blanket, in her jail cell that she might cling to in order to comfort her in her loss of her boys.

Susan's two attorneys portrayed her as a victim of mental illness to gain sympathy, even though they could not contend that she was insane at the time of the crime.

People grasp for an explanation that could ameliorate the guilt of Susan's family and that of her community. Before the trial, some media editorials called for the defense attorney to accept a plea bargain, but he refused. After the trial was over, newspaper editorials questioned again the defense attorney's insistence on a trial rather than a plea bargain arrangement, which would have spared the tens of thousands of dollars expended on the trial. But the editorials failed to note that if Susan had pled guilty, and thereby eliminated the trial expense, then only the judge would be involved in sentencing.

What was happening? Why did Susan's defense insist on a trial after Susan had confesssed already? If it was true, as the defense attorneys contended, that Susan was not insane and took full responsibility for what she did, why did the defense spend so much time and money on parading witnesses to speak about Susan's mental illness? Did Susan allow her attorneys to make their case, and indirectly, to try to gain sympathy. Was she trying again to perpetuate her "victim stance" in yet another manner?

Although Susan admitted that her carjacking/kidnapping story was a hoax and she confessed to killing her children, she still wanted to appear as a helpless victim of mental illness (as evidenced by her confession statement). This turned out to be a cleverly pragmatic ploy by her defense attorneys to avoid the death penalty for her. Clearly, by not pleading guilty, Susan let her defense attorneys weave a different, but confusing story of victimization.

In past history, there are tragic cases of treating psychotic individuals as though they were completely criminally responsible for all their bizarre actions. But today, the courts have often gone to the opposite extreme of letting genuine criminals off the hook by adhering to a theory that the person's environment or mental condition totally excuses them from any moral responsibility for their actions.

In the Harvey Milk murder trial in California, for example, the defense attorneys were successful in evading punishment for their client by invoking the theory that the murder was caused by his eating too many "Twinkie" cupcakes. The public perceived this "Twinkie defense" to be the last straw in involving a "victim mentality," an attempt to remove responsibility for criminal actions.

Although Susan Smith's defense attorneys stated that Susan accepted responsibility for her actions on the night of the crime, they, in fact, portrayed her as a "victim" of her dysfunctional family and sexual abuse.

When the victim mentality gets out of hand, as in the

"abuse excuse," it discredits the legitimate cases of true victims. Some forms of mental illness do render a perpetrator "insane" and therefore not responsible for his or her actions. But the abuse of using mental illness generally to excuse behavior runs the risk of undercutting public support for legitimate cases of insanity. If a person is not insane, then they are morally responsible for evil choices they make, choices that result in criminal actions. All human behavior is not simply determined by the person's heredity and/or environment. There is no scientific proof of such radical determinism—instead, determinism is just an unproven assumption that is sometimes useful in the work of science.

There is no excuse for killing one's own children when the court determines that the individual was sane at the time of the killing. Such was the case in Susan Smith's crime. The jury of twelve unanimously agreed on this point in rendering the double murder convictions after a careful evaluation of the evidence presented in court.

It was a difficult uphill climb for the prosecution to seek the death penalty for Susan Smith. Only one woman has been executed in the United States since 1976 when the U. S. Supreme Court reinstituted the death penalty. Only two women have been given the death penalty in South Carolina history. And no individual has been put to death in Union County.

On January 16, 1995, CNN's "TalkBack Live" broadcast focused on the issues of responsibility versus "victim stance." The emotional reactions of the public to the murder of the Smith children were reflected in the many opinions of both the invited guests and the studio audience. David Bruck, Susan Smith's lead defense attorney, described Susan's reactions. "She is lost in an ocean of grief and guilt and there is no relief; when she falls asleep, she has nightmares about her children in the water."

A member of the audience asked me whether there had been follow-up psychiatric evaluations of Susan Smith following her confession. I responded that, up to that time, the attorneys for Susan Smith had blocked any psychiatric evaluation. It was thus unclear whether Susan was now telling the truth or whether she was again manipulating the authorities for her own benefit.

Diane Rust-Tierney, the director of the Capital Punishment Project at the ACLU, was present as a panel member. She reviewed the personal problems of Susan from her early childhood and asked the rhetorical question, "Will [the death penalty] increase the pain or will it help the healing, and I submit that the death penalty under these circumstances can only increase the pain and impede the healing that must take place in Union, South Carolina."

But Ted Gogol, the Director of Operations at the Law Enforcement Alliance of America, took strong issue with Ms. Rust-Tierney's opinion. Gogol described the tragedy only in terms of the drowned children. "The highest moral principle in this nation in this world is human life, and to deny the proportionality of punishment to crime is to deny that dignity of human life. And we feel that it is entirely proper and absolutely moral to have a death penalty for heinous crimes such as this."

It was clear that in this microcosm of America, that there is much difference of opinion on the subject of capital punishment, and we are not closer to a consensus after the Susan Smith trial.

As a member of the panel, I described the several profiles of women who kill their children. Of the several profiles, there are two that are possible in the Susan Smith case: One is the possibility of a psychotic depression where a person is episodically psychotic with a major depression.

At that time they may be suicidal. Some of these women commit "suicide by proxy." They are in a confused mental state at the time of the crime. In South Carolina, if that is the case, the jury can find her "guilty but mentally ill," and she would go into treatment before serving a sentence, or she could be found "not guilty by reason of insanity." The other profile that she could fit is the revenging parent who has a retaliation motive against the husband and the father of the boys.

Since this television program, we have had the Susan Smith trial in which the defense strategy did raise the issue, by their choice of witnesses and line of questioning, as to how responsible Susan was due to her mental illness. It would be important for those in Union, South Carolina, and especially for her close family and friends, not to shift blame to themselves. After all, that seems to be the defense maneuver of Susan herself to try to make others feel guilty for what she has done wrong. That's the manipulative blame-shifting technique of taking on the "victim role."

As David Smith told Barbara Walters, on "20/20," "I want people to stop and remember her confession. Remember the gut feeling of what happened, and stop seeing her as a victim. Michael and Alex lost their lives. Michael and Alex were pure and innocent. They did nothing wrong."[17]

Susan's family and community sense the embarrassment of not getting Susan help at earlier warning signs. But predicting her type of violence is almost impossible and the public, and Susan herself, still grasp for an explanation for her unthinkable crime.

8

The Trial:
What was Susan's Motive?

During the weeks prior to the deaths of Alex and Michael Smith, communication accelerated between Susan Smith and her lover, Tom Findlay. Shortly before the October 25 murders of Alex and Michael, Susan wrote an undated handwritten letter to Mr. Findlay. This letter was entered into evidence on July 19 in her double murder trial:

Dear Tom,

Just a note to say thank you for everything. I could never express in words how much you mean to me. I will always treasure our friendship and all of the many wonderful memories we have made.

I want you to know that I have never felt with anyone, the way I feel when I'm with you. I have never felt so needed. You are a very special person and that is part of why making love to you is so wonderful.

I know how you feel about our relationship and I respect that. I'm appreciative of your honesty with me. I do want us to be friends forever and I'll never let anything happen that would change that.

I do hope that we will be able to date some and be together again someday, but if we never made love again, my feelings for you would not change because having you as my friend is worth more than sex could ever be worth.

Once again, I'm sorry for Sat. night and would take it back in a [heart-shaped design] beat if I could. I really wanted to be with you and hated that I wasn't.

Thank you for being there for me through all the rough times. You are a true friend. I want you to know that I will always love and care for you for the rest of my life. You are the best friend anyone could ever have.

Well, I hope I said everything right. The bottom line is: I'm glad we are friends and if that is all we can be, then we will just have to do a hell of a job of being that. Who knows what the future holds for our relationship. I'm just going to live one day at a time.

One more thing before I go, please don't ever hesitate to call me if you ever need anything! I will always be here for you!

> Friends Forever, [a heart-shaped
> design on each side of these words]
>
> Susan

A few days before Susan tragically killed her little boys, she received this reply from her lover, Tom Findlay:

Oct. 17, 1994

Dear Susan,

I hope you don't mind, but I think clearer when I am typing, so this letter is being written on my computer.

This is a difficult letter for me to write because I know how much you think of me. And I want you to know that I am flattered that you have such a high opinion of me. Susan, I value our friendship very much. You are one of the few people on this earth that I feel I can tell anything. You are intelligent, beautiful, sensitive, understanding, and possess many other wonderful qualities that I and many other men appreciate. You will, without a doubt, make some lucky man a great wife. But unfortunately, it won't be me.

Even though you think we have much in common, we are vastly different. We have been raised in two totally different environments, and therefore, think totally different. That's not to say that I was raised better than you or vice versa, it just means that we come from two different backgrounds.

When I started dating Laura, I knew our backgrounds were going to be a problem. Right before I graduated from Auburn University in 1990, I broke up with a girl (Alison) that I had been dating for over two years. I loved Alison very much and we were very compatible. Unfortunately, we wanted different things out of life. She wanted to get married and have children before the age of 28, and I did not. This conflict spurred our breakup, but we have remained friends through the years. After Alison, I was very hurt. I decided not to fall for anyone again until I was ready to make a long commitment.

For my first two years in Union, I dated very little. In fact, I can count the number of dates I had on one hand. But then Laura came along. We met at Conso, and I fell for her like "a ton of bricks." Things were great at first and remained good for a long time, but I knew deep in my heart that she was not the one for me. People tell me that when you find the person that you will want to spend the rest of your life with . . . you will know it. Well, even though I fell in love with Laura, I had my doubts about a long and lasting commitment, but I never said anything, and I eventually hurt her very, very deeply. I won't do that again.

Susan, I could really fall for you. You have so many endearing qualities about you, and I think that you are a terrific person. But like I have told you before, there are some things about you that aren't suited for me, and yes, I am speaking about your children. I'm sure that your kids are good kids, but it really wouldn't matter how good they may be . . . the fact is, I just don't want children. These feelings may change one day, but I doubt it. With all of the crazy, mixed-up things that take place in this world today, I just don't have the desire to bring another life into it. And I don't want to be responsible for anyone else's children, either. But I am very thankful that there are people like you who are not so selfish as I am, and don't mind bearing the responsibility of children. If everyone thought the way that I do, our species would eventually become extinct.

But our differences go far beyond the children issue. We are just two totally different people, and eventually, those differences would cause us to break up. Because I know myself so well, I am sure of this.

But don't be discouraged. There is someone out there for you. In fact, it's probably someone that you may not know at this time or that you may know, but would never expect. Either way, before you settle down with anyone again, there is something you need to do. Susan, because you got pregnant and married at such an early age, you missed out on much of your youth. I mean, one minute you were a kid, and the next minute you were having kids. Because I come from a place where everyone had the desire and the money to go to college, having the responsibility of children at such a young age is beyond my comprehension. Anyhow, my advice to you is to wait and be very choosy about your next relationship. I can see this may be a bit difficult for you because you are a bit boy crazy, but as the proverb states "good things come to those who wait." I am not saying you shouldn't go out and have a good time. In fact, I think you should do just that . . . have a good time and capture some of that youth that you missed out on. But just don't get seriously involved with anyone until you have done the things in life that you want to do, first. Then the rest will fall in place.

Susan, I am not mad at you about what happened this weekend. Actually, I am very thankful. As I told you, I was starting to let my heart warm up to the idea of us going out as more than friends. But seeing you kiss another man put things back into perspective. I remembered how I hurt Laura, and I won't let that happen again; and therefore, I can't let myself get close to you. We will always be friends, but our relationship will never go beyond that of friendship. And as for your relationship with B. Brown, of course you have to make your own decisions in life, but remember . . . you have to live with the consequences also. Everyone is held accountable for their actions, and I would hate for people to perceive you as an unreputable person. If you want to catch a nice guy like me one day, you have to act like a nice girl. And you know, nice girls don't sleep with married men. Besides, I want you to feel good about yourself, and I am afraid that if you sleep with B. Brown or any other married man for that matter, you will lose your self-respect. I know I did when we were messing around earlier this year. So please, think about your actions before you do anything you will regret. I care for you, but also care for Susan Brown and I would hate to see anyone get hurt. Susan may say that she wouldn't care [copy unintelligible] husband had an affair, but you and I know, that is not true.

Anyhow, as I have already told you, you are a very special person. And don't let anyone tell you or make you feel any different. I see so much potential in you, but only you can make it happen. Don't settle for mediocre in life, go for it all and only settle for the best . . . I do. I haven't told you this, but I am extremely proud of you for going to school. I am a firm believer in higher education, and once you obtain a degree from college, there is no stopping you. And don't let these idiot boys from Union make you feel like you are not capable or slow you down. After you graduate, you will be able to go anywhere you want in this world. And if you ever wanted to get a good job in Charlotte, my father is the right person to know. He and Koni know everyone who is anyone in the business world in Charlotte. And if I can ever help you with anything, don't hesitate to ask.

Well, this letter must come to an end. It is 11:50 p.m. and I am getting very sleepy. But I wanted to write you this letter because you are the one who is always making the effort for me, and I wanted to return the friendship. I've appreciated it when you have dropped me nice little notes, or cards, or the present at Christmas, and it is about time that I start putting a little effort into our friendship. Which reminds me, I thought long and hard about getting you something for your birthday, but I decided not to because I wasn't sure what you might think. Now I am sorry I didn't get you anything, so you can expect something from me at Christmas. But <u>do not</u> buy me anything for Christmas. All I want from you is a nice, sweet card . . . I'll cherish that more than any store (copy illegible) present.

Again, you will <u>always</u> have my friendship. And your friendship is one that I will always look upon with sincere affection.

Tom

p.s. It's late, so please don't count off for spelling or grammar.

A short week after receiving this letter from Tom Findlay, Susan Smith became the object of intensive national and international media coverage with the story that her children had been kidnapped by a black man who forcibly took her car from her. Reporters have claimed that no other news story on children has received so much national and international press attention since the Lindbergh child kidnapping case decades ago.

For the first nine days that Michael and Alex were reported missing, there was daily media coverage on the nationwide search for the two preschoolers. Susan and her husband David appeared on national television pleading for the return of their children.

When Susan confessed to killing her children, there was public outrage followed by extensive media coverage of her legal case and trial. Why?

The public perceived the murders as inconceivable. How could a mother tearfully claim, on national television, that her boys had been kidnapped, only to turn around nine days later and to confess that she herself had killed them?

The trial drew all the interest of a television "soap" drama with handsome characters with unthinkable deception, crass betrayal, and numerous lurid sexual liaisons. Sworn courtroom testimony detailed Susan Smith's sexual relations with Tom Findlay, and with her stepfather, Beverly Russell. In this case, truth seems stranger than fiction.

It is particularly baffling to imagine why a mother would mercilessly kill her own helpless little children. During Susan's trial, Tom Findlay testified that Susan made a comment wondering how her life might have been different if she had no children, and if she had not had children so young.[1] The seamy sexual affairs and suicidal gestures in Susan's story were cited as the critical factor in Judge William Howard's decision to ban television cameras from his courtroom.[2]

The basic question in the public's mind has been the question of Susan's motive—why did she do it? This is a question at the core of the fields of clinical psychology and psychiatry. Dr. Seymour Halleck, Professor of Psychiatry at the University of North Carolina, put it this way in his sworn testimony at Susan's trial: "The issue here is one of motivation. Psychiatry tries to understand motivation. We're not perfect at it, but it is the bread and butter of our business."

How can we understand a killer mom's mind? The public curiosity centers on the psychological dynamics of how a mother could murder her own cute little boys. There are subplots to the drama, including Susan's illicit lover, Tom Findlay, and her rejected handsome husband. There is the story line of her father's suicide, and her politically prominent stepfather who admitted to sexually abusing Susan.

By drawing from details from the story of Susan Smith's life and comparing those facts to the research on personality profiles of parents who kill their children, we can gain a glimpse into this killer mom's mind.

- Why did she do it?

- What pushed Susan Smith "over the edge"?

- Was Susan Smith a tragic victim or an unusual criminal murderer?

- Was she mentally ill or just plain evil? Or was the crime influenced both by her evil and her mental illness?

- Why did she offer lies and excuses?

- How can we understand a mother who killed her helpless little sons?

One place to start is to examine the words in Susan's written confession, witnessed by law enforcement officers.[3] On November 3, 1994, Susan wrote:

When I left my home on Tuesday, October 25, I was very emotionally distraught. . . . I felt I couldn't be a good mom anymore but I didn't want my children to grow up without a mom. I felt I had to end our lives to protect us all from any grief or harm. I had never felt so lonely and so sad in my entire life.

<u>I was in love with someone very much, but he
didn't love me, and never would</u>. I had a very difficult time accepting that. But I had hurt him very
much and I could see why he could never love me.
. . . I then got out of the car and stood by the car a
nervous wreck. Why was I feeling this way? Why
was everything so bad in my life? I had no answers
to these questions. I dropped to the lowest when I
allowed my children to go down that ramp into the
water without me. . . .

The next day, the owner of Conso Products, J. Cary
Findlay, posted a stern warning to his employees in the
hallways of the plant: "If you speak to the media about
Susan Smith or Tom Findlay, you will be fired.[4] Cary Findlay also hired extra guards to patrol the entrances of Conso
and his estate, and he hired a lawyer for his son[5] who
released this letter from Tom:

I am devastated by this tragedy. I cooperated
and have been cooperating with the legal authorities since last week in the disappearance of Susan
Smith's children. The only reason I am coming forward to issue this statement now is because of the
continuing inaccurate reports of my relationship
with Smith.

I did have a relationship with Ms. Smith and on
October 18 I told her that I was terminating that
relationship for a number of reasons and gave her a
copy of a letter to that effect, a letter which I gave
to the authorities early in this investigation. One of
the reasons for my termination of the relationship
was that I was not ready to assume the important
responsibilities of being a father.

However, that was far from the only reason for
terminating the relationship and certainly was not

the most important. At no time did I suggest to Ms. Smith that her children were the only obstacle in any potential relationship with her.

I know nothing about what happened that night or why it happened.

I intend to continue cooperating with the law-enforcement authorities in their investigation and I share in the grief of this community in the loss of the two children. I will make no further statements.

A next step in determining Susan's motive is to compare the facts of her case to the profiles of other mothers who have killed their children.[6] The research on these profiles is based upon in-depth interviews and studies of mothers after their court cases have already been settled and their participation in the research cannot further jeopardize their legal situation. These profiles were developed by examining the reported motives of the murdering mothers.

Four of the six basic profiles of parents who kill their children clearly do not fit Susan Smith, but the two other profiles can be considered for how well they fit the facts that have come out of the court proceedings:

The four profiles which clearly do not fit the Susan Smith case are these:

• **The Fatal Battered Child Profile** is where discipline goes wrong,[7] and a physically abusive beating goes too far and the child dies of injuries.[8] This clearly does not fit this case.

• **The Abandoned/Unwanted Child Profile** usually occurs shortly after birth where a baby is left in a trash can to die. Often, these are cases of extramarital paternity of the child. Alex was fourteen months of age and born to a married mother; also, Susan did not simply abandon, but guaranteed drowning for her sons, so this case does not apply to her.[9]

• **The Mercy Killing Profile** occurs when desperate parents resort to killing their child to relieve the child from some form of incurable suffering.[10] But for Susan, the Mercy Killing Syndrome does not fit the facts of the case.

• **The Psychotic Parent Profile.** Some mothers develop postpartum psychosis after the birth of a child, and others develop a postpartum depression, which is so severe that they experience psychotic features.[11] Was Susan psychotic at the time of the crime? The doctors who examined Susan did not report psychosis, and even her own defense attorneys concluded that there was no evidence for insanity. Susan demonstrated that she knew that drowning her children was wrong by concocting her phony story about the kidnapping of her children. For example, within minutes of killing her children, she was passing off her story regarding kidnapping by a black man, which she continued for nine days. Never once did she evidence lack of contact with reality of the sort found in psychotic patients.

The next two profiles can be compared to the evidence that came out of the trial:

• **The Suicide by Proxy Profile.** Was Susan Smith's crime actually Suicide by Proxy? Some parents become enmeshed with their child to such an extent that the boundaries between them and their children are blurred. When severely depressed, such a parent can become suicidal, and killing their child with whom they closely identify has been called Suicide by Proxy in the sense that the parent confuses the killing of her child with the killing of themselves.[12]

Susan claimed to have intended to kill herself together with her boys in the car, but she said she changed her mind while preparing the car to enter the lake. Susan did have two prior suicidal gestures in the past. Some of Susan's own confession seem to fit aspects of this profile, and her defense attorneys would have had reason to pursue this theory of Suicide by Proxy, but they did not. Also, the fact that Susan's children were male, not female, would weaken the case that she identified so closely with them. It is reasonable to expect that the psychiatrists and psychologist who examined Susan Smith for the state and for the defense were aware of this Suicide by Proxy profile, but they did not report finding this profile in the facts of their evaluations of her.

- **The Retaliating/Manipulating Parent Profile.** Revenge murders are perpetrated by mothers who want to manipulate the child's father to cause him permanent suffering by killing his children.[13] In such cases, it has been found that the children killed by mothers are almost always boys, and multiple children are usually killed at one time. Some of these mothers claim that their male children reminded them of their hated husband who fathered the boys.[14]

Susan's crime, in some respects, does not appear to have been a momentary impulse out of passion. Instead, she reports that she drove around for two-and-one-half hours contemplating what she would do. Then, she had to drive eight miles out of Union to the lake.

The other variation of this syndrome is the mother who wants to pose as a victim to gain the sympathy, love, and affection of a man she wants as a lover. Susan could be seen to have both the features of hostility toward her estranged husband David and the motive to pose as a victim to get her lover Tom's attention back. In fact, the prosecution based its arguments for a murder verdict on Susan's strong desire to restore her romantic relationship with Tom Findlay, the man whose romantic feelings for Susan had diminished and the one who saw her children as an absolute hindrance to their relationship.

The State of South Carolina opened its case against Susan Vaughan Smith by portraying her—as *The State* newspaper put it—"as a manipulative, evil woman whose children were in the way of her ambition. She had designs on the town's most eligible bachelor, Tom Findlay, who told her in writing he wasn't prepared for a ready-made family."[15] During Susan's trial, three of Susan's fellow employees at Conso, including her former lover, Tom Findlay, testified that Susan had at times told them that she wondered how her life would be different if she did not have her children.[16] The prosecution contended that Susan killed her two little boys because they were a stumbling block in a relationship with Findlay and she wanted them out of the way.[17] The assistant prosecutor in the case, Deputy 16th Circuit Solicitor Keith Giese, stated in his opening statement, "On the night of October 25, 1994, Ms. Smith removed that obstacle from her life. This is a case of selfishness. I, I, I. Me, me, me. That's the bottom line of this case."[18]

Susan rehearsed her fondest hopes for a blissful marriage at age nineteen, a marriage that had soured to the point of divorce proceedings that she herself had initiated earlier in 1994. And now, her rich lover/boyfriend, Tom Findlay, had just proven to be a bitter disappointment, after she had dreamed of a different kind of life free of money worries with him. Somehow, she could not live without male attention, yet every male had seemed to fail her, and repeatedly.

Under the surface of her outward friendliness, boiled the intensity of her anger and rage toward males in general and toward her estranged husband, David, in particular. Her young, handsome sons, Michael and Alex (consciously or unconsciously) reminded her of their father David and how she was trapped by that failed relationship. Now that she had filed for divorce, it so easily could have seemed that only Michael and Alex stood between her and a future with Tom. Somehow, her thoughts could have become excessively self-centered and full of self-pity. Only some dramatic crisis could possibly help her regain Tom's affectionate sympathy. Only the tragic absence of her two boys could make it possible for her to regain Tom's affection and caring. The responsibilities of single motherhood overwhelmed her. She desperately needed to be released from her burden. She reached for the parking brake to release it, then quickly and quietly shut the car door, which sealed it as a tomb for her little helpless and unsuspecting boys.

According to her own confession, on October 25, 1994, a deep feeling of lonely emptiness persistently haunted the twenty-three-year-old Susan Smith as she tried and tried again to focus on her routine office work. Perhaps it was the painful rejection she had recently experienced—a rejection she sensed was "final" this time—from her bachelor lover, the fun-seeking son of the wealthy owner of the Conso company. Tom's words in that one-week-old letter were, no doubt, still agonizingly fresh in her memory. Painful words in that epistle still seemed to slice right through her as they echoed in her mind, especially his frank explanation: "I'm not ready to become a father for Alex and Michael."

By posing as a victim of kidnapped children, who are eventually discovered dead, Susan had a chance to regain Tom Findlay's romantic attention, free of the obstacle of the children who seemed to stand in the way of Susan's one chance for a wealthy, jet set life. Prosecutor Giese insisted in court that the Susan Smith case centers on her long deception about what happened to her sons.

"For nine days . . . she begged the country to help find her children. She told us that she begged her God to help bring her children back to her safely. And the whole time, she knew they were laying dead at the bottom of John D. Long Lake," Giese said.[19]

Giese stated that Susan V. Smith knew right from wrong at the time of her crime, "She knew she made a decision that was wrong and yet she did it. Why?"

The motive, according to the state's case against Susan, was her desire for a continued relationship with Tom Findlay. Giese pointed to Tom's letter to Susan just one week before Susan drowned her children. That was the letter in which Tom stated that there was no future for their relationship, in part, because he was not ready to be a father to her children. As Giese spoke these words, Susan hung her head while one of her attorneys attempted to steady her.

Curiously, in response to this picture painted by the prosecutor, defense attorney Clarke straightforwardly admitted Susan's guilt in killing her boys. And Clarke, too, asked the jury to consider Smith's life, not just the days following the drowning. "We tell you about her life not to make you feel sorry for her but to gain your understanding."[20]

Clarke contended, "Susan Smith is not here to place blame on anyone else. She is not here to say, 'I am a victim.' "

"She is not here to say in any technical or legal sense that she was insane. She knew it was wrong to kill. She tried to cope with a failing life, and she snapped."

Clarke then painted a picture similar to the Suicide by Proxy Syndrome of parents who murder their children. She argued, "It was a failed suicide," referring to the night

Susan killed her boys. "Suicide is why we're here. She failed in her suicide and she lied. Susan's lies grew. Her lies to you. Her lies to me. Her lies to everyone in this courtroom. Her lies to everyone in this country were unforgivable. It was wrong and she is ashamed."

"The victims in this case were Michael and Alex Smith. They were beautiful children, precious children. They were loved by their mother. They were loved by their father. They were loved by all of us."

Many of the parents with this Retaliating Parent Syndrome have been found to have a *Borderline Personality Disorder.* The person with a borderline personality has a long-standing pattern of instability in emotions, in self-image, and in relating to others, together with a pronounced impulsiveness, which begins in early adulthood.

If a psychologist knew the background history and previous psychological and psychiatric evaluations of Susan Smith that were presented in her trial, and if that psychologist were performing a more comprehensive psychological evaluation of her to describe the dynamics of her personality, it would be reasonable to collect further assessment data to determine whether or not Susan has a borderline personality disorder or borderline personality traits. The borderline personality disorder is manifested in at least five of the following ways, and with each symptom pattern I have listed in parentheses some suggestive data from the trial that may fit each pattern:

1) making frantic attempts to avoid actual or imagined abandonment by another person (Susan's crime occurred one week after her rejection by her boyfriend Tom Findlay);

2) repeatedly developing intense but unstable relationships with others in which the person vacillates

between idealizing the other person and devaluing him or her (Susan reportedly vacillated this way in relation to her husband, David, and may have also "devalued" her sons with this dynamic);

3) persisting with a very unstable self-image, to the point of having an identity disturbance (Susan desired to escape her lower middle class status and desired a new life in the upper class by marrying her rich boss's son);

4) reacting very impulsively in a potentially self-damaging manner in more than one area of life (we could possibly view her multiple-partner promiscuity this way);

5) repeating self-mutilating behavior or suicidal gestures or threats (Susan had two prior suicidal gestures, and claimed to feel suicidal the night of her murders of her two sons);

6) regularly displaying highly unstable and shifting mood states, such as intense displeasure, irritability, or anxiety (Susan is reported to blow up with irritability and rage at her husband);

7) experiencing empty feelings repeatedly (Susan apparently was feeling this way the night of the murders);

8) having difficulty in controlling anger or displaying inappropriate strong anger, extreme sarcasm, enduring bitterness, or verbal outbursts—this anger is typically displayed when a lover is perceived as abandoning, withholding, neglecting, or being uncaring (we have described several instances of Susan's explosive anger);

9) temporary paranoid suspiciousness or dissociative symptoms under periods of stress (Dr. Halleck described some dissociative symptoms in Susan).

Some of these individuals develop psychotic-like symptoms during especially stressful times. Some of these individuals derive more security from "transitional objects" such as a pet or inanimate object. (In a letter from prison to her mother, published in the local press, Susan yearns for an object—such as a baby blanket of her son—to comfort her.)

The childhood backgrounds of adults with a Borderline Personality have greater frequencies of *sexual abuse*, neglect, physical abuse, *early parental loss or separation*, and *hostile family conflict* than the general population (the italicized features are found in Susan's history). Seventy-five percent of individuals with Borderline Personality are females. The prevalence of Borderline Personality is approximately 2 percent of the adult population.

Susan's motives have emerged more clearly from this evidence from her trial, but in light of her motive, stated desire to die, and her mental condition, what is the most appropriate sentence for her?

9

The Sentence: Mercy for a Depressed but Merciless Mother?

"Baby killer!"

"Murderer!"

"Shame! Shame!"

The deafening, hostile shouts clamored relentlessly at Susan Smith for those agonizing minutes while the sheriff and his deputies escorted her out of the Union County Courthouse to a police vehicle after her November 3, 1994, arrest for double murder. The immediate public reaction to Susan's shocking confession hardly smoldered at all before breaking out in the heat of consuming fiery flames. Outraged Union residents fiercely shouted for Susan to be sent to the electric chair.[1] Calls for swift revenge exploded all at once from the offended hearts of the vocal Union public.

The next day, I agreed to appear as the invited guest for a South Carolina TV news program. Callers again expressed sheer rage and revulsion toward Susan: Some demanded that she be strapped helplessly into a car, as she did to her boys, and rolled down the same boat ramp into John D. Long Lake, to be left to suffer a slow, suffocating drowning.

Reminiscent of the vigilante "justice" of the "Wild West," another caller proposed that Susan be released at the Union County Courthouse to see how far she could run through a gauntlet and still come out alive. The brutal, but perhaps realistic, prediction, of course, was that she would never make it out of the town limits alive.

On the TV broadcast, I tried my best to calmly distinguish between justice and revenge for the appalling child killings. I urged viewers to defer any judgment to the proper trial process. I interacted with callers about the dark evil of the actions Susan confessed to. We dialogued about how other stressed-out or depressed parents can draw from their social support network instead of isolating themselves and thereby leaving themselves vulnerable to dark urges and temptations.

This discussion appeared to be helpful in calming down callers. It seemed to help promote a civilized consideration of right and wrong, and the need for prevention as well as for justice. I attempted to convince the TV viewers to think things through more rationally, and to focus on everyone's constitutional and basic human rights.

But when I was about to leave the broadcast studio, the TV station told me that they had just received another phone call asking to speak to me at the station. An irate woman viewer protested that I was *too calm!* She chided me for not assuming the same feverish pitch that the callers had. She wrongly assumed that I must not have any children myself to speak so calmly about this case!

Ironically, Susan herself expressed a preference to receive the death penalty so she could be "reunited with

1. Susan Smith with Sheriff Howard Wells, on right, leaves the courtroom after receiving guilty verdict of double murder. Photo by Boyzell Hosey/The State

2. Beverly Russell leaves the courthouse after testifying in defense of his stepdaughter, Susan Smith. Photo by Pam Royal/The State

3. Tom Findlay, on right, on the day he testified in Susan Smith's trial. Photo by Perry Baker/The State

4. David Smith holds up photo of his sons that he wore each day during the trial of Susan Smith. Photo by Pam Royal/The State

5. Susan Smith's car slowly sinks into John D. Long Lake in the prosecution's re-enactment of the crime that killed her two boys. Photo by Jamie Francis/The State

6. The Monarch intersection not far from downtown Union where Susan Smith said a black man jumped into her car as she stopped for a red light. Photo by Steven G. Rekers

7. A view down Main Street in the small old town of Union, South Carolina. Photo by Steven G. Rekers

8. A TV news broadcasting satellite dish in front of the Union County Courthouse where the Susan Smith double murder trial was held in July 1995. Photo by Steven G. Rekers

9. The portable stages for TV news broadcasting directly across the street from the front of the Union County Courthouse where the Susan Smith double murder trial was held in July 1995. Photo by Steven G. Rekers

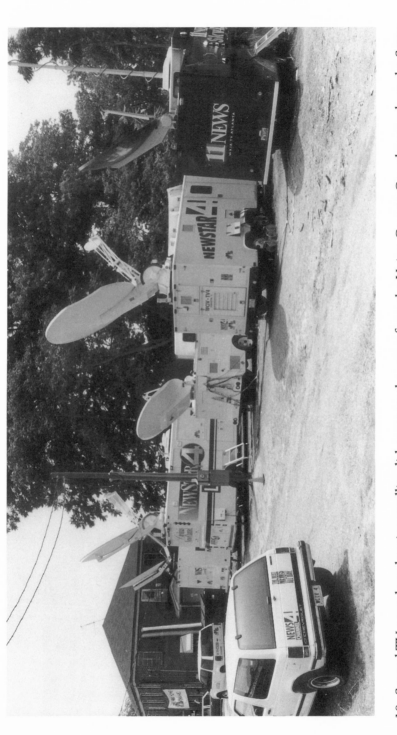

10. Several TV news broadcasting satellite dishes across the street from the Union County Courthouse where the Susan Smith double murder trial was held. Photo by Steven G. Rekers

11. The Union County Courthouse where the Susan Smith double murder trial was held. Photo by Steven G. Rekers

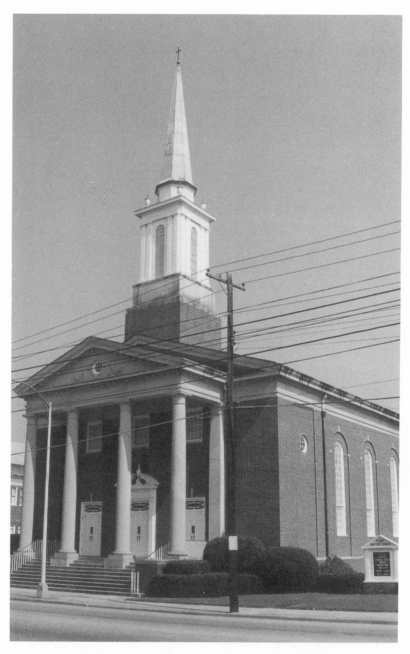

12. The First Baptist Church of Union where Sheriff Howard Wells took Susan Smith for an interrogation that resulted in her confession that she killed her two boys. Photo by Steven G. Rekers

13. The memorial to Michael and Alex Smith next to the boat ramp of the John D. Long Lake. Photo by Steven G. Rekers

14. Visitors left flowers and toys in memory of the two children.
Photo by Steven G. Rekers

her sons." In the Women's Correctional Institution in Columbia awaiting her trial, Susan met once a month with her pastor, the Rev. Mark Long of Buffalo United Methodist Church. The day Susan's pre-trial court proceedings began, the local media carried quotes of an interview with Pastor Long who said, "If she had her druthers, she would prefer death than to spend thirty years in prison because the thought of her children would be on her mind."[2] She did not anticipate peace of mind while living through the rest of her life.

Since Susan's confession, the people of Union have urgently sought understanding of what happened at the lake on October 25 in order to decide what corrective action could restore their sense of genuine justice. Tragically, the ordinary people of Union polarized themselves between those backing the death penalty for Susan[3] and those opposed to administering that ultimate punishment. Grocery store chitchat, office conversation, and private musings in homes weighed the increasing information about Susan conveyed by the news media. The community choices urgently faced are: What does Susan deserve?

Psychiatric care?

Prison?

Or the death penalty?

After Susan V. Smith was found guilty of two counts of murder on Saturday, July, 22, 1995, the penalty phase of her trial began on Monday, July 24.

If you had been on Susan's jury, how would you have sentenced a merciless, but depressed former mother?

Because this was a high profile trial, many people were interviewed regarding their opinions on how Susan should have been treated by the court. In light of these community opinions, Susan's history, and the court evidence discussed in previous chapters, you can weigh all the evidence as if you were a member of the jury.

To come to your own decision, you will need to address these kinds of questions:

- Is Susan Smith morally responsible for murdering her children?

- Is there ever any excuse for killing your children, such as the "abuse excuse"?

- Is anyone who kills his or her own defenseless little children actually "insane" by definition? Why did the defense attorneys and the defense lawyer indicate that Susan was sane at the time of the crime?

- What was Susan Smith's motive for killing her two helpless sons?

- What difference did it make that Susan Smith and her defense attorneys refused to simply plead "guilty"? Why did they force a full trial? Why did they present mountains of testimony about Susan's mental illness and suicidal gestures, even though they were officially denying a "victim stance" and officially denying that they were making excuses for her killing her children?

- Was Susan Smith really a mentally ill victim or an evil criminal when she killed her boys?

- Is Susan Smith mentally ill but still responsible for drowning her children?

- Does Susan Smith deserve sympathy or punishment for her crime?

- Should courts grant mercy to a merciless mother?

- If you were on the jury, would your verdict be:
  Not Guilty
  Not Guilty by Reason of Insanity
  Guilty but Mentally Ill
  Guilty of Double Murder

- Did Susan Smith deserve psychiatric care, prison, or the death penalty for drowning her children?

Because Judge William Howard banned cameras from the courtroom for the Susan Smith trial, most of the public could not watch the rapid, tense "soap opera-like" drama which occurred on this legal "stage." So let's paint a word picture of the courtroom so you can vividly imagine yourself seated on one of the two pews in the jury box.

The Union County Courthouse, with its semicircular entrance with eight stately pillars is a most impressive structure. The original courthouse was built in 1822, designed by South Carolina architect, Robert Mills, who also designed the Washington Monument. The court was rebuilt on the same granite foundation of its predecessor between 1911 to 1913, at a cost of $60,000.[4]

Renovated in 1974, this courthouse contains all the county government offices for Union county, including the sheriff's office in the basement where Susan had been interrogated many times during the nine days before her belated confession. The second-floor courtroom happens to be one of the largest in South Carolina, which proved to be convenient for such a high-profile case which attracted so many news reporters.[5]

If you were a member of the jury, you would be escorted into the courthouse from a side entrance, coming out of a van, which took you from the hotel in which you were sequestered from your family and friends for the duration of the trial. (Mercifully, Judge Howard kept the trial down to two weeks total, sparing jury members prolonged isolation—typical for South Carolina.)

If, on the other hand, you were a member of the general public or the press, you would climb up the steps at the front of the courthouse, enter past several guards at the front of the building, and enter into the foyer of the first floor. Security was unusually tight after the town had experienced the "vigilante" mob scene surrounding Susan's arrest.

Two curved oak staircases lead to the second floor courtroom. Entering the rear of the courtroom from an entrance to your right, you would observe a long rectangular dimly-lit room about 120 feet long and 60 feet wide with large windows along the right-hand wall—windows that face the rear of the building. On the center of the front wall is a coin-shaped plaque measuring about four feet in diameter. It reads, "Union County Court • Union, SC."

Four law enforcement officers stand guard at the front of the public audience section, and two stand guard at the back of the room. Guards also stand outside each entrance. There were dozens of law enforcement officers standing guard throughout the entire courthouse for this "media event" trial.

These police went into swift action on the second day of the trial on July 18, when the court received a bomb threat, requiring that everyone swiftly exit the building for the rest of the day. A myriad of officers searched the courthouse but found no bomb. The next day in court, the first order of business was to arraign a man in an orange prison outfit whose phone had been traced with special security equipment as the originator of the bomb threat call.

In the right front corner of the room is the jury box. In the center front is the judge's elevated bench with the witness stand on the right side of the judge's bench as you face the front of the courtroom.

The Clerk of the Court has a desk immediately in front of the judge. In front of the clerk's desk on the left is the defense table where Susan Smith and her two attorneys, David Bruck and Judy Clarke sit. A parallel table on the right is the prosecution table, where the young lawyers Tommy Pope and Keith Giese, sit.

A four-foot high partition divides this front part of the courtroom from the thirteen rows of public seating. Only an opening in the center of the partition allows witnesses to come from the public seating up to the witness stand.

The thirteen pew bench rows are filled with the members of the press and the public. The first two rows on the left-hand side are reserved for Susan Smith's family and friends, while the first rows on the right side are reserved for David Smith's family and friends. In total, there were approximately 175 people observing the first day of the trial, and about 154 people observing the second day. But as the two week trial progressed, the full 200 plus spaces were completely filled, until the last half of the trial saw crowds of people turned away who had hoped to get a seat to observe the proceedings.

Even though microphones were used at the witness stand and in locations for the attorneys to stand, the acoustics were not very good in the old courtroom, and when attorneys strayed from their microphones to make a dramatic point, or when a witness leaned back, it was difficult to hear what was said. Any movement on the old creaky floor would drown out the voices at the front, so Judge William Howard enforced a strict order for the public not to move from their seat while he was on the bench.

Of course, if you were on the jury, you would have the best seats to hear everything spoken in the front of the room. When videos were shown to the jury, the monitors faced their box only, and the judge had to leave his seat to watch. The viewing public could not see the videos, although they could hear the soundtrack. So the courtroom spectators could not see the video of Susan's pleas on TV for the return of her children by the "kidnapper," or the video of the re-enactment of the six minute sinking of Susan's Mazda Protégé into the John D. Long Lake.

Before, during, and after the trial, the public heatedly discussed what would be an appropriate sentence for confessed double murderer, Susan Smith.

For example, the "Mail" section of letters to the editor of a major magazine, included a comment about Susan's defense attorney's characterization of the death penalty as "cold-blooded . . . premeditatedly setting about to exterminate people." One response in reply said, "What exactly did his client do if not set out premeditatedly to murder her two sons?"[6]

The letters to the editor page of a national magazine contained this comment on the appropriate penalty for Susan Smith: "Life in prison or the death penalty? I am outraged! The death penalty was written for Susan Smith."[7]

Susan broke down when the prosecutor read the indictment of murder charges against her. She buried her face in her hands and sobbed as she heard the prosecutors confirm the charges. Did her reaction suggest that she was genuinely remorseful and thus should not receive the death penalty for the murders of her two young sons, Michael and Alex?

One older resident of the rural community said, "I don't believe that taking her life is going to accomplish anything at all. I think she is already suffering every day."

A woman overhearing this remark replied, "But she needs to pay for what she has done."

Someone else asked, "You mean she ought to be executed?"

"Yes," the woman answered.

A boy on the sidewalk chimed in, "I'll tell you what. Every day the prison guards should show her a video of her little boys playing and then show her a video of their bodies that were recovered from the lake to make her remember the horrible things she did."

The publisher of an area newspaper was asked, "What was the reaction of the community in Union when the prosecutor announced that he would seek the death penalty in this case?"

"Well, there was a mixed reaction depending upon who you talked to. A lot of the women with small children were in favor of the death penalty. But the men tend to be more lenient and would go along with a life sentence."

Susan's experiences in jail before her trial were anything but pleasant. The jury learned from Dr. Seymour Halleck, that Susan was and is currently suicidal.[8] She sits in her jail cell that always has a light on so she can be monitored twenty-four hours a day by closed-circuit television cameras. She has been somewhat in isolation, although she gets some short visits from family members who are carefully monitored during the visit. She is allowed some reading materials and she gets an exercise period.

Before and during her trial, Susan received special treatment by the prison authorities, special visitations, a paper gown, and some special meals. She was also closely guarded. Returning to the prison after receiving the life sentence, Susan asked a guard, "Does this mean that I will be treated just like all the other prisoners now?" The reply came quickly, "Yes, Susan. We cannot unfairly discriminate against anyone, and we have to treat you like all the others now that you are no longer presumed innocent, but have been found guilty."

David Bruck, Susan Smith's attorney, who has made a career of opposing the death penalty, made a public statement before Susan's trial: "The death penalty for her is beside the point. She says over and over again that she wishes she could just die so that she wouldn't hurt anymore."

Along these same lines, Susan Smith's brother, Scotty Vaughan, explained, "Susan's pain is in living, not in the fear of dying. I don't think the state could punish her any more than she's been punished."

Members of the public at large have expressed a variety of strong opinions about Susan Smith. One observer thought that an important dimension had been overlooked:

> It's not a matter of whether Susan deserves the death penalty. The question is, "What is the proper punishment for her crime?" The media has reported that Susan is from a God-fearing family. If so, she must be aware of the fact that there is a Creator and all of us will have to face Him after we leave this form of life. I would hate to be in her shoes as she faces God Almighty for what she did to two of His creatures that were lovingly made in His own image.

Another South Carolinian agreed with the above sentiment and added his own thoughts,

> I think this country is bent on too much violence. Our children kill in neighborhoods. We kill in wars. I think Susan is really sick for killing her own kids. I think we need to go into her mind and find

out why she did it. Then we can heal and we can get the country to heal. I don't think that putting people to death is the answer to anything.

But there have been many opinions expressed from throughout the country.[9] Here are a few:

"Susan Smith should get the death penalty for one reason—her children did not have a choice. They are innocent and their life was taken away."

"Nothing excuses murder, especially murder of little children. The emotional distress Susan experienced is very common. We need to protect our kids first and foremost. Time has a way to lessen pain so life in prison will fade as a reminder of her guilt. I believe in the death penalty, and it's appropriate for Susan Smith."

"I think the death penalty is too good for her. In this case I think it would be a reward instead of punishment. I think she should have to stay in a small cell for the rest of her life, paying for what she did."

"I do believe in the death penalty. Some people feel Susan has to live for the next sixty years, replaying this tragedy every day in her mind as her punishment. But consider the cost of sixty years of incarceration to the taxpayers. How many college educations would that pay for?"

"If she lives out her life and has to replay and think about this every day, is this so much worse than dying?"

"The only way to come back to the moral principle of retribution, rather than revenge, is to recognize that humans are causal agents who are responsible. Humans are freethinking and have a moral being. Because of that, we have free choice. Susan Smith made that decision to murder her children cold-bloodedly and in a horrific suffering way."

"Vengeance is not supposed to be a reason for execution, but it seems to be the only reason in this case."

"As you grow up your mother is a sure protection for you as a child. I was shocked to hear someone say that because Susan was allegedly abused, that it is okay to kill children."

Death penalty cases are not swift because American society respects the law. We don't want to make an error in sending a criminal to execution. Because of the finality of the death penalty, if our justice system is going to use it, the American people would want to be assured that we applied it to the right person. One of our safeguards is the legal appeals process, which can take up to ten years for a death penalty case.

Under the U.S. Constitution, the American system cannot render a death penalty on one day and the execution the next day. That happened in a South American country in a case where a mother was found guilty of killing her little children by bashing their heads in order to clear the way for a romance with a young man. The day of her guilty verdict, she was promptly hanged. But this could never occur under the United States justice system.

There has been much discussion of the death penalty itself. Not surprisingly, many people seem interested in the relative costs of the death penalty versus life imprisonment.

Would it be less expensive to execute a child murderer than to keep her alive for sixty years? Because of the constitutional safeguards, plus a cumbersome legal process, death penalty cases in our country are very expensive. It often turns out to be more costly to execute an individual than to provide them life in prison. In New York and Texas, it costs around 1.5 million dollars per death penalty case. In Florida, it costs about 2.5 million dollars.

In spite of the costs of law enforcement and court cases, many point to the principle and to the practical need for a more effective justice system: "In America, violent crime is out of control. Murder rates are higher than ever before. We must get a better handle on this significant problem." Many believe that the criminal justice system in this country has been taken over by smooth-talking lawyers making excuses.

We do not have proportionality of punishment if we don't have the death penalty, and the absence of the death penalty denies the dignity and moral value of a human life.

The death penalty divided and polarized the people in Union, just as it has the nation.[10]

In Union some believe that the healing process has started. Each person will come to his or her own way of having closure with this trauma.

The thought process regarding the appropriateness of capital punishment can be clarified by making a distinction between vengeance and justice. The American people recognize moral absolutes. If the court process finds that a killer was not mentally ill at the time of the crime, he or she could fit the revenge profile: This is where the mothers kill more than one child, the mother tends to kill a male because the male reminds them of the father, and the mother has the motive of trying to permanently damage the spouse or manipulating to get a lover's attention by killing her own children. That is morally evil.

The public should not think that all psychologists and psychiatrists lack moral standards just because they identify some psychotic people as out of touch with reality.[11]

After all the prosecution and defense witnesses had presented their testimony in Susan Smith's trial, the judge sent the jury out and addressed Susan herself:

"You have the right to testify yourself. And you have the right to remain silent. Have you discussed this with your attorneys, David Bruck and Judy Clarke?"

"Yes," Susan acknowledged.

"If you exercise your right to remain silent, I will tell the jury not to take it against you," the judge continued. "I want to make sure it's your decision. It must be your decision alone. Is it your decision not to testify?"

"Yes, sir," Susan said quietly.

The judge continued, "No one else has told you that you cannot testify?"

"No."

Then Judge Howard asked for the jury to come in, and he informed them that the evidence part of the trial was concluded and they would need to return at 2 p.m.

Then the judge and attorneys discussed the charges against Susan. The judge said, "We have a statement in evidence by the defendant that she let the car go into the water. Her intention for unlawful action is malice. The jury could reasonably conclude that the defendant is guilty of a crime."

". . . on the issue of the suicide attempt, suicide is a felony, raising the inference of malice."

Then the judge responded to a memorandum from Mr. Bruck proposing the lesser charge of manslaughter. He stated that we have a situation where a person voluntarily got out of the car, released the brake of the car with the children strapped in. He asked Mr. Bruck, "Is there any basis that the jury can say it's unintentioned?"

Mr. Bruck said, "The court is overlooking the testimony of Dr. Halleck."

"Isn't it based on hearsay," the judge replied.

"She told him that she backed out of suicide. Behind the homicidal intent was the suicidal intent. . . ." Mr. Bruck said.

"You say, 'She got out of the car, and immediately [backed out of suicide]'. . . .then there is no further purpose to kill the children," the judge noted.

In their further discussion, the judge asked this of Mr.

Bruck: "Suppose I drive my car with you in it, and I drive it at 100 miles per hour in order to kill myself and you. Suppose at the last moment I change my mind, and I am the only one to survive. Is there any basis to say I am only guilty of involuntary manslaughter?"

Mr. Bruck argued that what is relevant is Susan's awareness of the situation at the time, and that Dr. Halleck had genuine doubt if she was aware at that moment due to her turmoil and confusion, and thus she leaves her children in the car. He argued this may be reckless but not malicious.

To this, Mr. Keith Geise argued, "That would be like a person who shoots a gun and after the bullet is on its course toward the person, he changes his mind. Susan set the events in course after letting go of the car's brake. Once she started the car in motion, she is responsible for the consequences after that. Her children were trapped in the car."

"Further, suicide or attempted suicide is a felony, and involuntary manslaughter requires that the person not be in the process of committing a felony. She was doing an unlawful act [if she was planning suicide]. She set into action an unlawful act."

"If a person is blowing up trees with bombs, that is a felony. In the process, if they happen to kill a child, that person is guilty of murder."

The judge pointed out that the "wheels were set in motion" by Susan, both figuratively and literally when she released the brake of the car. But he nevertheless allowed the jury to consider involuntary manslaughter on Mr. Bruck's theory.

Tommy Pope addressed the jury:
"The defendant is charged with murder. The charge is that Susan Smith with malice of forethought murdered

Michael Smith by drowning. The second charge is that she did kill Alexander Smith with malice, with wickedness, and lack of social duty, and Alex died of drowning.

". . . [the defense lawyers] admit she did it. They say she was not insane that night. They say she knew what she did was wrong. She confessed."

Referring to the defense's psychiatrist, Dr. Halleck, Mr. Pope reminded the jury, "He said she could conform her conduct. . . . he danced on suicide as the reason why Susan killed Michael and Alex." He reminded the jury that Dr. Halleck agreed, on cross-examination, that ". . .if I decide to commit suicide and if I take you with me, it is murder."

Mr. Pope reminded the jury that he had asked the defense's psychiatrist, "Did Susan Smith intend to kill her children?" and Dr. Halleck said, "Yes."

He reminded the jury that all this came from the defense's own expert.

Mr. Pope told the jury that the judge would define malice for them as mischief, not caring, lacking social duty to another. He argued that a prime example of social duty is to protect your children. And Susan Smith chose affirmatively not to protect her children at John D. Long Lake.

"The judge will tell you that suicide is a felony. So you can infer malice while an act is committed in the process of the commission of a felony. Even if you believe what she was intending was to commit suicide, she killed the boys in the process," and that fulfills the legal definition of malice.

". . . she said she had her hands over her ears so she couldn't hear her babies crying for her and their father."

". . . why didn't she go to the [McCloud] house and say, 'Oh my God, I almost committed suicide, and my babies are in there'?

"Why did she bail out of the car to stop her suicide? All she had to do is pull the brake, which she had done two times just before. She knew the brake worked. Why didn't she do that?"

"At the McClouds, her clothes were not torn. Her clothes were not wet. Susan had made no attempt to rescue her children after letting the car roll down the boat ramp. Smith, you just don't make sense!"

Then, Mr. Pope reviewed the statements of witnesses regarding the relationship between Susan and Tom Findlay. He quoted Susan's supervisor, Sandra Williams, as reporting that shortly before the children's disappearance, Susan had told her that she was in love with Tom, but they couldn't be together because of the children.

Mr. Pope quoted from Tom's letter to Susan the week before, which said the children were an obstacle to their intimate relationship. Pope quoted other witnesses who reported that Susan said, "Sometimes I wonder what my life would be like without kids," just shortly before the murders.

And Mr. Pope reviewed the multiple attempts Susan made to warm up her romantic relationship with Tom the day of the children's deaths. Each attempt failed.

He reminded the jury that Susan showed up at the McClouds in Tom's sweat shirt, and she made no reference to a "botched suicide." And then the first thing Susan said to Tom when he calls to offer sympathy over her missing children is an apology for offending him. At that moment, Susan's two little boys are dead at the bottom of the lake. "Shouldn't we be a tad more concerned about the kids?" Mr. Pope asked.

Mr. Pope also reminded the jury that during the nine days that Susan perpetrated the kidnapping hoax, blaming a black man for the disappearance of her boys, she sent word for Tom Findlay to come to her, but Tom never came. "This tells us what this woman is truly thinking," Mr. Pope argued.

Then Susan told Agent Logan on November 1, 1994—seven days after killing her boys— "If I had one wish, I would wish that I could turn back time and not have told Tom Findlay that I had sex with his father." Pope concluded, "Tom Findlay in her mind is the reason." He noted that Susan talks about "me" and "I" in her confession, and even mentions her desire for Tom as she describes how she killed her boys.

Pope reminded the jury of the question, "Why did Susan Smith not just give her kids to someone else?" And he provided a basis for his answer: "The reason she doesn't give up the boys is because she won't have Tom Findlay."

"If Susan went to the [McCloud] house and says I almost committed suicide, then she's not a victim. But if she drives to Monarch and gets kidnapped, now *she's* the victim. She has opportunity to get rid of the kids and have Tom Findlay. The only fallacy of that plan was, [it turned out after all that] Tom Findlay never came."

"Is she guilty or not guilty? Her own expert said Susan intended to do it. On the night of October 25, 1994, Susan Smith made a choice, a horrible, horrible choice. She chose the love of another man over her boys. She wasn't depressed that night. Her own doctor said her boys gave her unconditional love and she only became depressed when alone."

"That choice of hers was something her boys never had as they were screaming and crying in that car. Like Michael and Alex screamed, this case screams out for the verdict of murder!"

Defense attorney Judy Clarke gave closing arguments for the defense. "We could not be further apart. . . .It is sadness that brings us together. . . . This is not a case about evil but a case of sadness and despair. Susan had choices in life but her choices were irrational and her choices were tragic."

"The only two people that loved her unconditionally are dead. She made a terrible decision with a confused mind and a heart without hope. Hopelessness is not malice."

"If Susan allowed the car to go into the lake because of a failed suicide, it may be murder or involuntary homicide. It's intent. If intent is malice, it is murder. . . . If intent is recklessness, it is manslaughter."

"Did she do it for Tom Findlay? He was part of the despair, not the goal, not the reason to throw away the most precious people in her life."

". . . I suppose, 'Please have Tom call me,' is evidence for murder. . . . She told the police about Tom Findlay. Well, that's real smart if that's the motive for murder. . . .Dr. Halleck was asked, "Was Tom Findlay the motive?" and he answered, "It's absolutely absurd."

"The lie. . . . What does it prove? It was wrong and inexcusable. She misled us, you and me, on a wild goose chase. Because we couldn't believe a mother could kill her kids, could it be she couldn't either?" This is not a rational, normal mind.

"Susan decided her life is meaningless. She decides to kill herself and she's going to take her children. 'I felt I had to take us to keep us from harm.' She went to the ramp to commit suicide and take her children. But failed. It's a very childlike response to the ultimate failure of life."

". . . I've got to tell you evilness [sic] had nothing to do with this. It had everything to say about mental illness. Dr. Halleck, with forty-three years of treating emotions said. . . 'If she had been on medication that night, we probably wouldn't be here.' Was it a failed suicide? I have to say, yes."

Ms. Clarke traced Susan's childhood, including her father's suicide, and her troubled years as a youngster. She brought up the incestuous relationship with her step-father, and her hospitalization at age eighteen for a suicidal attempt and depression. She reviewed Susan's fears of her husband David tapping her phone and finding out about her affairs to make them public.

Ms. Clarke then painted a picture of Susan as a "de-spairing young woman." ". . . I think you can see she snapped." ". . . if it's depression, it's involuntary manslaugh-ter. Did the state meet the burden of proof to show she is evil and wicked, or a despairing, alone, troubled, helpless child that she was that night?"

In his instructions to the jury, Judge Howard defined murder as "the unlawful killing of any person with malice of forethought." He clarified that malice is "the intentional performance of an unlawful act with intent of harm," and it "suggests hatred, wickedness, intent to do wrong." "If a person takes the life of an innocent person, malice can be inferred." He said that malice need not exist for any partic-ular length of time to render it murder.

He defined "criminal intent" as "intention to violate law. . . a mental state of conscious wrongdoing." Judge Howard also clarified that "to undertake to do suicide is unlawful."

The jury weighed all the evidence and rejected the defense attorney's theories and unanimously found Susan Smith guilty of two counts of murder, which required finding malice, not just recklessness.

If you were on Susan Smith's jury, what would it be? A life sentence (carrying an automatic eligibility for parole in thirty years in South Carolina), or the death penalty?

The jury in Union unanimously voted to give Susan Smith a life sentence. One juror had temporarily urged the death penalty because of Susan's nine days of cover-up lies to the media, but he reconsidered and joined the majority.

In a media interview, the jury foreman stated that he thought a life sentence was more punishment than a death penalty would be. Some on the jury expressed the feeling that capital punishment would come too soon and be too good for Susan. When one juror was interviewed on a television program, he was asked what he thought about Susan Smith being released from prison in thirty years as allowed in this sentence. He replied, "That's a scary thought."

The jury may have been influenced by all the attention given during the trial to Susan's desire to die. They may have not wanted to give her what she wanted.

In South Carolina, a person sentenced to execution now has a choice between the electric chair and lethal injection. Although it was a possible outcome in Susan Smith's double murder trial, it was never very likely that she would face execution. No matter how repulsive or heinous the crime is, if it is committed by a woman, the odds are minuscule that execution would be the penalty in the United States.

Watt Espy, the former head of the Capital Punishment Research Project at the University of Alabama, reported that only one percent of the 2000 women who commit murder annually are sentenced to die. But then more than 98 percent of those sentences are later overturned in appeals.[12] That would mean that on the average, fewer than one out of the 2000 women who murder annually are eventually executed. Another way to look at the statistics is this: about 13 percent of all murders are committed by women, and yet less than 1 percent of people on death row today are women.

Velma Barfield was executed for murder by North Carolina in 1984. She was the only woman who has been executed in the United States since the death penalty was reinstituted in 1973. No woman has been executed in South Carolina since 1947 when a woman was sent to the electric chair for bludgeoning her husband to death. Of the 18,808 legal executions recorded in the United States since 1608, only 514 were women—that's less than 3 percent.[13]

But in the intervening eight months between the boys' deaths and the trial, press reports indicated that increasing local union majorities came to prefer a life sentence over a death penalty for their community's most famous, or infamous citizen.[14] Some Union citizens expressed the argument that a life sentence without parole would be the most appropriate and severe punishment.

David Smith strongly objects to the "victim stance" taken by Susan and her defense attorneys. He feels that the real victims—Michael and Alex—seem to have been lost in the discussion of how Susan was victimized by her stepfather and others. His book, *Beyond All Reason*, was written to remind the world that the lives of Michael and Alex

. . . were ended in a horrible act of selfishness. As the weeks and months go by since they were murdered, I find myself more and more frustrated. Somehow, the focus has slipped away from them, the real victims in this terrible story.

When I hear the lawyers talking, when I hear them holding Susan Smith up as a 'victim,' it makes me angry. For myself, I would have rather stayed silent. But for Michael and Alex, I feel I have to speak."[15]

On television David expressed disappointment for the life sentence Susan received, a sentence allowing for parole in thirty years. Some said that fifteen years of prison per child cheapens the worth of a child's life.

David discussed his visit with Susan in jail before her trial, a visit which helped him clarify his feeling regarding the best punishment for Susan. She had requested that he come to see her, and he reluctantly agreed.

"When I walked in the room, Susan was sitting with her back to me. We made eye contact. It was a feeling I couldn't express. Everything went cold."

"We began to hug. She was crying.

"Did you ask her why she did this?"

"I had to keep asking [why she did this]. I was deeply soul-searching. She said, 'I don't know why.' "When I asked her, 'Why didn't you give me the kids?' she said, 'I don't know.'"

"When I said, 'I didn't know you cared so much about Tom,' she said, 'I don't know why.' "

The day Susan's trial ended, I was asked, "Is it possible that Susan Smith doesn't know why she killed the kids?"

I noted that if the prosecution's view is correct that Susan's motive was to recover her romantic relationship with Tom Findlay, then it would be extremely difficult for her to admit she was so selfish as to sacrifice her own kids for an adulterous relationship. It is such a universally recognized evil motive, that who would want to admit to it? So it is not surprising that she offers no other explanation, and says, "I don't know" instead as a way of exercising the psychological defense maneuver of "denial." Or two other defense maneuvers are possible here: With such an unacceptably evil intent, it is possible that her unconscious mind "represses" the thought of the motive. Or that her conscious mind deliberately puts the extremely uncomfortable thought out of her mind, thereby "suppressing" the motive.

Susan is sentenced to at least thirty years in prison, at which time she will be eligible for parole. She will be fifty-three years old at the time of her earliest date of release from behind bars.

10

The Recovery: Is Healing Possible for Susan, Her Family, and Union?

Since the tragic murders of Michael and Alex Smith, many profoundly practical questions have been asked:

- How can the boys' father, David Smith, and his extended family cope with the excruciating pain and irreplaceable loss of being robbed of Michael and Alex?

- What are the possibilities, if any, for restoration of their murderer, Susan Smith?

- How can Susan's family recover?

- What will bring about the healing of the community of Union?

The Susan Smith story vividly portrays many of the common dilemmas that the human race has grappled with down through history. This is one reason why the Smith story has been so gripping to people all over the world.

171

These common human dilemmas reached painful crescendos in Susan's life. Susan's murderous actions created horrendous suffering to others around her. In an extremely intensified way, Susan Smith and those she affected have faced the same basic psychological, existential, and spiritual questions everyone encounters at one time or another:

- What is it inside of me that causes me to do the very things I don't want to do?
- What should I do with these dark feelings inside me?
- What am I to do with myself when I don't live up to my own ethical standards?
- How can I deal with the pain of the past or the present?
- How can I overcome feelings of inadequacy and low self-worth?
- How can I cope with the many difficult stresses in my life?
- How can I handle all of my children's needs?
- How can I cope when I feel overwhelmed?
- Why am I so restless for more after I reach a valued goal?
- With all the uncertainty in life, is there anything out there that I can count on any more?
- When I see so much injustice happen, is there a way for justice to ultimately prevail?
- How can I have more than disappointing or superficial relationships?
- What should I do if I feel I am desperately at the last straw?

- When the bottom drops out in life—tragedy, disaster or death—where can I turn?

As if the above questions were not enough to grapple with, newspaper, radio, and television news reporters have raised a number of additional profound and weighty questions pertaining to healing for the community and for Susan's family:

- What community resources are, or should be, available for a mother who is feeling at the end of her rope?

- Is there any light at the end of the tunnel for Susan's family?

- Is forgiveness of Susan's murder of her two little boys necessary, or even possible, by David, by her family, and by the community of Union?

- What does the Smith's church teach about forgiveness?

- How does forgiveness work? That is, what is the psychology of forgiving another person?

- Is it necessary for Susan to admit her guilt and to repent so that forgiveness is possible? If Susan persists in the defenses of making excuses, rationalizing her actions, taking a victim stance, and/or continuing to lie about aspects of her killing of her own children, is forgiveness by anyone possible or desirable? Isn't it an insult to forgive someone who does not admit to being wrong in a matter, and who does not turn from that wrong?

If Susan could ever change from her horrific criminal condition and self-destructive lifestyle:

her *unthinkable selfishness* (see Chapter 1) would need to be replaced by *genuine, dependable, self-sacrificing love for others;*

her *repeated preoccupation with suicide* as a "solution" when life gets tough (see Chapter 2) would need to be replaced by a *genuinely worthy reason to live life* in all circumstances;

her *voluntary incestuous life* after age eighteen (see Chapter 3) would need to be replaced by *purity of family affection;*

her *chronic infidelity* (see chapter 4) would need to be replaced by a loyalty to one individual;

her *crass betrayal* (see Chapter 5) would need to be replaced by *courageous, self-sacrificing loyalty;*

her *deceptive "victim mentality" and manipulative lying* (see Chapter 6) would need to be replaced with the dignity of *living with the truth of her own human responsibility* for her own actions;

her tendency to offer *belated confessions only when trapped* by her own duplicity (see Chapter 7) would need to be replaced by *telling the truth and spontaneously and rapidly repenting* the wrongdoing;

her *evil manipulation* (see Chapter 8) would need to be replaced by *genuine self-giving service for others;* and

her *mercilessness* (see Chapter 9) would need to be replaced by *gracious protective care and mercy* toward others.

That would be a massive personality transformation! A tall order indeed! It is no surprise that some think it impossible to accomplish, and that others contend that only God Himself could cause such a massive transformation and change of heart.[1]

But think what a difference it would make, not only for Susan's life, but for those around her, if such change were possible by any means, whether it be psychological or spiritual. But before any such personality change is possible, Susan must first recognize and admit to the core source of her problems.

The evidence presented in her trial indicated that Susan had been aware for a long time that she has major personal problems. What has been Susan's main burden all her life? What is it that deeply concerned her? What caused her personal anguish and suffering? And has she even begun to understand the core problems that underlie her emotional and relational problems? These are the final questions to consider about Susan Smith herself.

Partly because Susan received a life sentence, we shall see that how Susan chooses to address her own problems can have a bearing on how those who know her are able to cope with what she has done to them.

Susan's deepest emotional suffering involved important relationships that disappointed her. First, it was her father who committed suicide when she was only six years old. Then, when she was fifteen, it was her mother who may have failed to protect her from continued incestual abuse possibly because she had higher personal and family priorities than Susan's well-being. Then, it seemed disappointment came in every relationship she had with a man. One of the psychiatrists who evaluated her after she committed the double murders said that Susan displayed one of the most severe cases of dependent personality disorder that he had ever diagnosed.[2] She has spent much of her life desperately seeking people on whom she could depend for emotional support, guidance, and affection. This was one result of her family upbringing.

Furthermore, for much of her life, and especially on October 25, 1994, Susan had the awful feeling that something was basically wrong all about her. She felt, "Something is desperately wrong with my world. It's not like it should be. Something is really messed up. And something is wrong inside of me."

This, in itself, is not an unusual observation. In fact, down through history, it has been a very common observation that something is profoundly wrong with humankind. Today, the daily news keeps reminding us that our world just isn't as it should be. We all get this uneasy feeling that something is out of place in the world. In particular, something is out of place in human relationships. It's not only in government, but also with your friends, with your neighbors, with people you know at school or at work, and even in your family.

And even closer to home, when we are very honest with ourselves, each of us notices that we don't consistently live up to our own conscience. There's something wrong inside. We can't get away from the uneasy feeling that something basic is really wrong with the human race and begs for a genuine solution. Susan Smith's life is a rather extreme example of the general capacity of the entire human race to suffer evil, to recognize their own dark side, and to do cruel and evil deeds.

In light of her double murder, her deceptive cover-up, and her adult life full of infidelity, it is not unreasonable to ask, "Is there any ray of hope for Susan herself? Is reformation possible, and does it seem likely for this convicted murderer?"

To answer these questions, I have had numerous conversations with the people and community leaders inside and outside of Union County in South Carolina. They have repeatedly pointed to some profound psychological and spiritual truths, which are at the heart of the desperate needs experienced by Susan Smith. Pastors and those in the lay community alike have pointed to a set of deeper core needs in Susan's life, needs that lie beneath her surface problems that are readily observable.

In this part of the country it is not surprising that Susan's condition would be commonly discussed in terms of Christian thought. The name of Susan Smith's home town, Union, was named for a church building that, historically, had been shared by several denominations. The state of South Carolina is deeply in the "Bible Belt" of America, where its citizens enjoy a strong religious faith. South Carolina, among the fifty states, has one of the highest percentages of the population with membership in Christian churches, particularly the Baptist and Methodist churches. So it is impossible to speak with too many people in Union or elsewhere in the state without entering into a discussion of the moral and spiritual implications of what Susan Smith did to her sons.

On July 9, 1995, the Sunday before jury selection began for Susan Smith's trial, many of the pastors in Union preached on the subject of forgiveness and Christian love before parishioners who could be called to jury service.[3] Newspapers carried the story that the local ministerial group, several individual pastors, and others in the community demonstrated their opposition to the death penalty by sending letters to Solicitor Tommy Pope.

Susan Smith's own pastor, the Rev. Mark Long of Buffalo United Methodist Church in Union, preached, "If we cannot love those who are unlovable, then we cannot expect to be loved by God."

The Rev. A. L. Brackett, pastor of the St. Paul Baptist Church in Union, told his all-black congregation, "If she's [mentally ill], take her to the hospital. If she's not sick, then punish her, but don't take her life."

The Rev. Thomas Currie of First Presbyterian Church in Union told a news interviewer, "Susan's emotional and mental state makes her responsible for what she did. But not death-penalty responsible."[4]

But the biggest news in the area papers on July 10 was the account by the Rev. Mark Long of Susan Smith's recent prison conversion to Jesus Christ. Pastor Long knew Susan as someone who occasionally attended his church. He had ministered to her three times at her stepfather and mother's house during the nine days Susan perpetrated the hoax of the kidnapping of her children.

News reports had quoted Susan as using Christian language and referring to prayer to God during that nine-day period when she posed as the victim of a carjacker who kidnapped her children. For example, on October 27, 1994, Susan is quoted as telling Gary Henderson, a news reporter for the Spartanburg *Herald-Journal*, "All I can do now is trust in the Lord and my family. I keep trying not to lose hope, but the more time passes, I get scared."[5]

But in retrospect, Pastor Long explained this religious talk by Susan this way, "Even though she didn't attend worship often, she was still familiar with the Biblical language of the faith. And she had received some spiritual counseling in high school from Pastor Tom Curie of First Presbyterian Church in Union."[6] So she was familiar with Christian vocabulary and could use it, even in a deceptive way. Her religious experience, to that time in her life, could better be explained in social and psychological terms,[7] rather than reflecting a genuine spiritual relationship with God.

The Rev. Long had also been one of four ministers who officiated at the funeral of Michael and Alex Smith in November 1994. Two weeks after the boys' funeral, he received a phone call from Rick Holiday, the chaplain at the Women's Correctional Facility in Columbia. "Susan wants you to be her minister in prison."

Long's first few visits with Susan were in the prison's administration building. She was brought in chains to a room in that building to talk with him. For all the monthly visits after that, Pastor Long was escorted to meet Susan in a maximum security area. There, the prison officials had to clear out all the other prisoners first, and then two guards led her down to the area in which Pastor Long was already waiting.

In his first meetings with her, Susan "was deeply depressed and talked a lot about dying. She was suicidal. After we talked, we prayed."[8] Pastor Long knew that Susan had been brought up in the church as a child, but her attendance as an adult was very sporadic. Between June 1994 and the time of her crime in late October 1994, Pastor Long had seen Susan in his small church only "three or four times."

In prison, Pastor Long patiently counseled Susan regarding her guilt and her spiritual need for a genuine relationship with God.[9] The unconditional love of his pastoral relationship with her made a deep impression on her, and she was open to his help.[10] Then after she had been in prison three months and Long had visited her several times, Long observed, "The Holy Spirit finally got through to her and she knew it was right." Seeking a personal relationship with God and the personal peace and healing from her weighty guilt, Susan prayed to receive full forgiveness by God.

During his subsequent visits with Susan, Pastor Long noticed that Susan would talk about her conversion to Christ, and she wanted to be baptized.

Susan's lead defense attorney, David Bruck, permitted Pastor Long to reveal this quiet jailhouse Christian conversion and baptism to the press in the days just before the opening of Susan's trial. *The State* newspaper quoted Long as commenting at that time, "I don't think the world knowing of her Christian conversion will save her life, but it might help."[11]

Many people in South Carolina expressed skepticism regarding Susan's timing for her "Christian conversion" in the weeks between her arrest for double murder and her death penalty trial. It seemed too "convenient" and useful for Susan's present plight of facing trial. Was this yet another manipulation to gain the affection and sympathy of others? Further doubts were raised regarding the genuineness of this apparent "jailhouse conversion"[12] when her defense attorney sanctioned the release of that information in the days just immediately prior to the jury selection phase of her trial.

The public wondered: Is this a genuine conversion to Christianity? Or is it merely a superficial "jailhouse conversion" calculated to elicit sympathy by the jury? Was Susan merely grasping at straws to decrease the sharp pain of her massive guilt? How can we tell the difference? What are the marks of a genuine conversion?

If her conversion is genuine, what are its implications? If it is not genuine, how can we recognize its phoniness? If this conversion is genuine, how will it affect Susan's mental illness? Will it affect her criminal nature? What impact could it have on the community of Union?

Since the guilty verdict for double murder, Susan has been strongly confronted by her moral guilt if she were not before. And "guilt" has been described as a place where religious faith and psychology meet.[13] So, was Susan using the minister's visits as a psychological tool to help her feel less guilty, or was there a genuine spiritual transformation taking place in her life? This is a key question to investigate to understand how Susan is functioning as a person now while she is in prison.

I listened intently to South Carolina's religious leaders when they discussed Susan Smith's core needs and conversion experience. I came away with four principles, which seem to summarize everything I've been told. These four principles can help us understand what is involved in Christian conversion and how Susan could genuinely have become coverted while in prison. I have attempted to translate these spiritual principles into contemporary psychological words and concepts[14] to faithfully convey what South Carolina clergy are saying about Susan's foundational personal needs and her current progress in spiritual growth and faith development:[15]

There is a crucial relationship Susan is supposed to have

Once Susan had confessed and found herself locked in a solitary jail cell for a few months, she became very aware that something quite significant was missing that could make her life better. Her life story indicates that she often thought, "Someone is missing. Someone I need. But I don't know who it is."

She was looking for one "anchor relationship" that she could never lose. In the deep recesses of her mind, she had an unmet desire, "I need someone who could love me ugly, as well as beautiful, and who will love me forever." She wanted a genuinely loving relationship that would not go away. She had lost a father, a best friend, and a lover. And she was at odds with her young husband. And she craved someone to love her who would always be there for her.

Because of the loss of her beloved father as a little girl, Susan felt this vacant emptiness much more keenly than most people do.[16] And tragically, Susan's whole life had been spent looking in all the wrong places for that one nondisappointing relationship.

Over the years, Susan had tried to find that relationship through a boyfriend or a romantic lover, and at first she would be on "cloud nine," and it would seem, "this is it!" But as time went on, disappointment would return. That gnawing feeling slowly would sneak back that says, "No, this is still not it." The boyfriend just could not fill the empty spot in her heart. And her depressing loneliness would come back in full force.

It is a clear consensus among the clergy I interviewed, that it is a very common human experience to have this feeling, "Someone is missing. I know someone is missing, but I don't know who it is." So we are all, at some time or another, looking for that one "anchor relationship" that we can count on never losing—one that will never disappoint us. This has been a universal human craving. It's like a "missing person" problem in our lives, but we don't know exactly who it is that is missing.

Some people try to solve it by having a close "best friend." Others accumulate lots of friends. Still others try to find that "missing person" relationship by having a really close-knit family. But eventually, if totally honest, they all realize that one certain someone is *still* missing. The one they sense they're made for.

This desire for a permanent loving relationship is not unique to Susan. She only felt it more keenly because of her dependent personality.

Why do people get this "missing person" feeling in their lives? That question is a deeply philosophical as well as psychological issue.[17]

Simply put, there's two basic possibilities to account for this universal need for a nondisappointing relationship.

On the one hand, some philosophers contend that we humans are here on planet earth as a result of pre-existing energy or matter, plus time, plus chance. This means we live in a universe that is basically, at its core, essentially impersonal. Therefore, our personalities evolved by chance from matter, and ultimately, our inner sense of needing one nondisappointing anchor relationship is a cruel mirage with no real solution. If this is the case—if we evolved from an impersonal universe—any search for a nondisappointing relationship just leads us down a dead-end path because every human being you might get to know will eventually disappoint you.

On the other hand, a more common and more satisfying answer to explaining the human need for a nondisappointing relationship is one that is described by Dr. Wendell Estep, Pastor of the First Baptist Church of Columbia —a church regarded by many as the historic flagship church for South Carolina.

> We were created by a very personal God who created everything by Himself and for Himself (Colossians 1:15-16). We know this is the case because God went out of his way to leave us a message in the Bible that says, "The whole Bible [is] . . . from God and is useful to teach us what is true and to make us realize what is wrong in our lives (2 Timothy 3:16). That Bible says that God created human beings to have personalities that reflect his personality (Genesis 1:27) and God intends that we have a full and meaningful life (John 10:10). So, this gnawing awareness that we need this one permanent, nondisappointing, "anchor"relationship is real and there is a real solution to it.

> The Bible says God has set "eternity" in all of our hearts (Ecclesiastes 3:11)—this is something like a "hole" inside us which only that one lasting "anchor relationship" can fill. That "anchor relationship" is meant to be God. Only an eternal God can fill this eternal vacuum inside each person's life.

> This "hole inside" can become more obvious to

us at the times when life is hard. We can see this to be the case, in an exaggerated way at times, in Susan Smith's life. Like Susan, each of us [is] more apt to recognize our need for that special someone's love and caring companionship when we are struggling with one of the common human dilemmas that give us a hard time.

A sense of emptiness and "cosmic loneliness" results when you lack that one nondisappointing relationship— that one totally fulfilling relationship, which can fill the void you feel. This is the core "spiritual diagnosis,"[18] that South Carolina pastors offer to explain the very common spiritual need that Susan Smith suffered prior to and at the time of her crime. Pastor Estep explains the historic teaching of the Christian faith in this regard:

> Nobody here on earth could possibly fill the eternity-sized "hole" in your heart. But God can. God loves us and wants to be our one "anchor relationship." The Bible tells us, "God so loved the world that he gave his one and only Son, that whoever believes in him shall not perish but have eternal life" (John 3:16).
>
> Jesus said, "I have come that they may have life, and have it to the full" (John 10:10b). Because God is eternal and has placed an "eternity-sized hole" in us, his initiative is to offer us a lasting relationship with him called "eternal life." As the Bible puts it, ". . .the gift of God is eternal life . . . ." (Romans 6:23).
>
> Greatly overshadowing the central issue during her trial—would she get a life or death sentence—is Susan Smith's core need to have *eternal life.*

The relationship Susan was supposed to have,
she didn't have

Susan had a feeling of uneasiness that something was out of place. Her relationships weren't working quite right. Her marriage seemed unsatisfactory so she was in the process of getting divorced. Her parents did not completely understand her. Nothing permanently satisfied her. She thought, "Every time I get what I think I need, I'm still left dissatisfied and wanting something more." She was not content with her life.

Susan was restless. She had what Ron Hutchcraft calls, "destination sickness": I got to my destination, and now I want another one. When John D. Rockefeller was asked how much money is enough, he said, "A little bit more."

Susan was the same way. When she had one relationship with a man, she still sought another one. She was never fully satisfied.

Why is more never enough? What's her problem? The clergy analyze it like this: Susan had a vacuum in her heart that no earth stuff could satisfy (Ecclesiastes 3:11 says God has put "eternity" in your heart). Earth is not eternity stuff. Susan was an achieving person who did well, but she had a vacant spot in her heart. So she was still restless.

The clergy also pointed to this: Susan, like all of us, was created for God, but living for "me." She was running her own life on her own terms when the personal God of the universe was supposed to be in charge of her life. Susan, like all people at some time or another, had made the choice that amounts to saying, "God, you run the universe, and I'll run my own life." Church leaders point to this attitude and lifestyle as what the Bible calls "sin."

Now, as a result of that basic choice to run her own life, Susan made a thousand "I'll be God" choices. In essence, she would live her life in such a way that she was saying, "God, I know you said 'tell the truth,' but in this particular situation, that'll cost me too much, so I'm going to lie my way out." So we saw the kidnapping hoax. That was an "I'll be God" choice.

"I know, God, you said, 'sex is for marriage' but, thank you, I want to do it tonight with this warm, affectionate guy, even though I'm not married to him." So we saw her extramarital affairs revealed in court. That, too, is an "I'll be God" choice.

"I know you said, 'do not lie,' but with the way things are happening to me, watch what I'm going to say to get what I want." So we heard testimony regarding Susan's lies to many people to try to have her own way. That's another "I'll be God" choice.

"I know you said, 'do not murder,' but I want to escape the situation I feel trapped in." Whether you believe the prosecution's contention that Susan planned to kill her sons to remove an impediment to her romance with Tom Findlay, or whether you believe the defense contention that it was a "botched suicide/double murder" plan, you have an extreme "I'll be God" choice in either case. It is widely recognized that taking another's life or taking your own life is "playing God."

Susan learned that the "animal" inside is selfish and prone to hurt the people she loved the most. The Rev. Ron Hutchcraft explains this age-old human irony from the words of the Apostle Paul in Romans 7, "The things I want to do I don't do. The things I don't want to do I keep doing." Susan, too, was scared about the dark thoughts she had when alone.

Susan was struggling with her failures. She knew she had failed, and she had this nagging sense that she didn't know how to clean up the mess she had left in others' lives and her own life.[19] Everyone has been the victim and the victimizer. Susan's life seemed to have a greater share of being victimized herself and then victimizing others.

The historic teaching of Susan's denomination is that a lifetime of the "I'll be God" approach of sin results in a tragic spiritual penalty—a kind of "death penalty." How can this death penalty be paid? Only by someone dying. The person themselves must suffer the spiritual death penalty, unless someone can rescue them by paying their penalty so God will have them back again.

And repeatedly, Susan's conscience would let her know she had done the wrong thing, and she felt deeply guilty. A pastor pointed to this practical truth: ". . .since they show that the requirements of the law are written on their hearts, their consciences also bearing witness, and their thoughts now accusing, now even defending them (Romans 2:15)." This kind of guilt induced by her conscience, as Dr. Halleck had testified in her trial, generated depression for Susan.

Those "I'll be God" choices are serious. In essence, what Susan did is push the *real* God away from her life, and put herself in his place. She wanted to run her own life, because she thought it would turn out better that way. But ironically, in doing so, she drove a wedge between herself and that one "anchor relationship" she was made for.

Her sinful nature produced hostility toward God, which created a barrier to her relationship with Him. The Bible says, "The sinful mind is hostile to God. It does not submit to God's law, nor can it do so. Those controlled by the sinful nature cannot please God" (Romans 8:7-8).

Susan's church teaches this: When God created her, He wanted to be her anchor relationship and He wanted to give her his loving companionship. But Susan's "I'll be God" choices—her sin—separated her from God (see

Isaiah 59:2) and she tragically pushed him, and everything he offered her, out of her life. And even worse, her sin caused her to be at odds with the best friend she could ever have. She did not truly understand that it is very serious for us to alienate the most powerful person in the universe.

On the one hand, if we are a product of energy or matter plus time plus chance, then when our body dies, that's the end of our existence. In that case, if Susan had received the death penalty, she would cease to exist as a person. But on the other hand, if we are in fact created by a personal God and the Bible is truly a record of his personal message to us, then when our body dies, our soul continues to live on forever, because we are created with "eternity" inside us.

By pushing God out of her life, Susan was excluding the source of everything good. It is no wonder, from this perspective, that everything seemed to be going so badly for Susan, as her written confession stated. If Susan were to continue in that direction, the final result is tragic enough in this life, but even more disastrous in the long run, because she would end up being separated forever from that one relationship that she sensed she needed.

It is not surprising that during the weeks between the time of her arrest for double murder and her death penalty trial, that Susan Smith would turn her mind to ultimate questions. There was a very real possibility that she could have been executed. Her attorney, Mr. Bruck, and her pastor, the Rev. Long, both opposed the death penalty and were speaking with her regularly about what they were doing to spare her life. The chaplains and minister with whom she spoke in prison also reminded her of her church's teaching that when our bodies die, our existence drastically changes.

If Susan had lived her entire life with an "I'll be God"

attitude, once she died (by execution or otherwise), her religion tells us that she would be trapped forever in that decision. She feared that if she committed suicide, that she would be separated from God forever in hell, and for years she feared that her father did not go to heaven because he took his own life.[20]

God gives everyone a real choice to run his or her own life, but once our physical body's life is over, our soul lives on. And our "I'll be God" attitude totally separates us forever from God and his good benefits. As she grew up, Susan had been taught that hell is where God forever removes every good benefit from one's life because he separates himself irrevocably from that person. In other words, God warns us that our "I'll be God" choices bring his judgment. According to Susan's church the built-in penalty for excluding God from control of one's life is to lose the one relationship we have all been made for— "The wages [or cost of that decision] is death [in other words, separation from God] (Romans 6:23).

The sinful "I'll be God" choice automatically results in two kinds of separation, in the teaching of Susan's church: The first kind is separation from God, called "spiritual death" is a result of God's perfect character which, by definition, cannot intimately relate to the imperfection of sin in a person. The second kind is the separation of the person's spirit from their bodies, called "physical death." It was physical death that Susan's attorneys and pastor were trying to prevent for her. But her chaplains and minister were reminding her of an even more serious form of death— "spiritual death" which she already was experiencing to some degree in her life.

The relationship Susan is supposed to have,
she doesn't have, but she can have

When you look at all the religions of the world, it can be seen that people from different cultures recognize that the world is an imperfect place. They then devise their own solutions to attempt to solve this universal human problem of guilt and their remoteness from God.

Susan's church teaches that it is a personal rescuer that is needed to save individuals in such a situation. Pastor Estep expressed it this way:

> The Bible teaches us that Jesus Christ is God and that he became a man to come live among the human race (John 1:1, 14).

The relationship Susan is supposed to have, that she doesn't have, but she can have, she must choose to have

Susan painfully knew that a one-way relationship cannot last indefinitely. She had a one-way romantic relationship with Tom Findlay in October 1994, and she repeatedly tried to find a way to restore it to a two-way romance. She told her supervisor at Conso Products that she loved a person who did not love her in return. That was emotionally painful for her, as it would be for anyone. A one-way relationship is eventually a dead-end relationship, because for a relationship to develop real depth, it must function both ways.

In prison, Susan learned that she was being like that with God. He was reaching out to her with His love in many ways. Maybe it's a beautiful sunset, a beautiful day, the birth of her children, her health, or the blessing of her life itself. But she was the one not returning the love. In his visits to her, Pastor Mark Long reminded her that God reached out with an offer to forgive her "I'll be God" sinful way of living through what Jesus Christ had done for her on the cross.

In speaking about the possibility of having a relationship with God, pastors often point to John 1:12: "Yet to all who received him [Jesus Christ], to those who believed in his name, he gave the right to become children of God."

But while sitting in prison, Susan was reminded by her ministers that for all her life, it has been a one-way relationship between her and God. It was God who had been doing all the loving, and to that point there had been no loving response back from Susan. All the while she was living with the "I'll be God" attitude.

But Susan's "I'll be God" attitude had gotten her into a horrendous mess. She felt depressed when alone and sometimes suicidal, according to Dr. Halleck.[21] But this was not something new for her; she had felt this way before and had received psychiatric help in a nearby hospital. She knew where that help was available, but she chose not to seek it. There are many concerned clergy in Union, but she did not turn to them. She had even turned down genuine offers of her husband, her family, and her friends to help her on the very day of her crime.

Susan had been making a sequence of ever-worsening decisions, until she made that terrible choice at John D. Long Lake. Her life couldn't be any worse than sitting in prison awaiting her death penalty trial for murdering her own little boys. Susan had run her own life and had made just about the biggest tragic mess anyone could get into.

In this context, it is not so surprising that Susan would be open to something different. All she could think of was suicide as a way out. But her chaplains and minister were suggesting a superior option: She could choose to accept God's offer of a relationship on His terms.

How could she make this new choice? The choice would involve a life-changing decision. It would be like driving south on a highway and suddenly realizing that you're headed exactly in the wrong direction. It's a fact of life that you can't drive north and south at the same time. You've got to turn from driving south in order to go north. So you've got to make a U-turn to correct your course. Now this isn't necessarily a two step process—you're actually turning from the wrong direction in the process of turning to the right direction.

The historic Christian faith uses the word "repent" to refer to this kind of "U-turn" in life: "Repent and turn to God and your sins will be wiped away" (Acts 3:19). Susan recognized that she had all the junk of her life—all those "I'll be God" choices about what she had done with her mouth and her body. All those "I'll be God" choices had been deadly serious. In fact, she had been a rebel against the God who made her. True conversion would require a turning away from that sin; in other words, she had to decide, "I've got to drop all this junk to turn to God through Jesus."

In sorting out whether Susan's prison conversion was genuine or not, it is essential to point out that repentance is not just feeling sorry for your "I'll be God" attitude, or feeling sorry for the mess you got yourself into by sinning.

Imagine every sin that Susan ever committed being written on a large blackboard. Her church teaches that if she truly "repents" and turns toward God, all her sins will be wiped away. Imagine then, God taking a huge eraser and completely erasing the entire list of her sins for which she deserves punishment, including lying to the public about what happened to Michael and Alex, adultery with Tom Findlay, adulthood incest with Beverly Russell, and the murders of Michael and Alex Smith.

Susan certainly does not deserve such forgiveness, but her church teaches that being rescued from the tragic condition of being separated from God (being "saved") is not something that can be earned or deserved, "For it is by grace you have been saved, through faith—and this not from ourselves, it is the gift of God" (Ephesians 2:8).

I asked Pastor Long, "Was Susan truly repentant when you spoke to her about this in prison?" He confidently replied, "She knew she received absolution from God."

In Christian teaching, *faith* and *repentance* are closely linked: If you were in a hurry to reach your intended direction and you truly *believed* that your driving south is the wrong way, you would do something differently—you would turn the car around and drive north. Sincere belief in the fact that your intended destination is located to the north is not enough to get you there. You also have to demonstrate your faith in that fact by turning around and driving in the opposite direction.

So genuine Christian faith can be observed by the direction the person is going in their life. This suggests that if Susan's Christian conversion is genuine, that it will have observable effects in the way she lives her life from now on. Time will tell.

Susan's church teaches about the kind of belief that is needed to be rescued, and it has something to do with your heart, not just your head.

Can it be faked? Yes, some people take the teachings of a minister and string along a series of words in a prayer, which is just words but not the person's honest desires. Others just tell someone that they prayed such a prayer when they were alone, when they had not really done so.

Pastor Long recognizes that some may think that Susan's reaching out to God in this way is merely a "jail-time conversion," but he says, "I think its authentic because she focused on her *life*," whereas previously, she was focus-ing on her suicidal desires to die.

Growing up, Susan had been raised in a church tradi-tion in which many believe they can pray and become converted, but later fall away and lose their salvation.

These people believe that a person can convert and gain salvation, then fall away, and reconvert, many times over a lifetime. Whatever their state, "saved" or "not saved" at the time of their death would determine their eternal destiny.

But in Susan's case, the minister was convinced that Susan had never genuinely been converted to Christ in the past, although she had a religious background and participated in religious activities. Susan's conversion in prison seemed genuine to the Rev. Long, so he agreed to her request to be baptized.[22] He baptized her there in the prison warden's office, which is in a space that is actually a remodeled prison cell.[23]

"This woman has lived in a real emotional cesspool all her life. It is almost as though, in her mind, suicide is the way out if her burdens are too much. It's what her father did," Long observed. "She had been crying out for help all her life."

"By July 5," Pastor Long observed, "Susan came to the resolution that she was ready to die." But Long drew a careful distinction between "wanting to die and being ready to die." Susan was coming to grips with her own mortality, like a terminally ill patient can do.[24] Instead of "wanting to die" in a suicidal way, "she was speaking as a person of faith, being prepared to face God in her judgment." This was a step for her own "sense of healing," her pastor said.

So when she faced her trial, she was "prepared for whatever the jury decides, even if it's death,"[25] as her pastor explained to the news media in early July. "If they decide she's guilty and want to execute her, she feels like she's strong enough now to accept that."[26]

"Susan knows she is forgiven by God," Long said. "But she is struggling with the next step of forgiving herself." Now that the trial is over, Long will continue to help Susan deal with these kinds of issues in living, in contrast

to her prior wish to die to escape her conflicts and burdens. "Now there's a sense of life in her. It has to do with
how she will persevere through this and how she . . . can
find a sense of worth."[27]

She will need to grapple with what it has been inside
of her that caused her to do the very things she didn't
really want to do. Pastor Long noted that he never came to
a resolution with Susan as to why she let her children go
into the lake. "It's as though it is blocked out of her mind."
A dilemma for Susan is that she seems to be "two kinds of
people," according to Long. On the one hand, she is a murderous person who allowed her children to die. But on the
other hand, she had loved them, defended them, and had
been tremendously patient with them. So it is hard for
Susan and others to understand how a patient and caring
mother, on the one hand, could let her children die, on the
other hand.

Susan contemplated suicide (like her father did), and
said she feared that she was not a good mother. She did
not want her boys to grow up without a mother, and with
"poor theology and with thinking that is not rational," (as
her minister, the Rev. Mark Long, put it), she let them die,
believing they would have less pain living in heaven with
God.[28] Susan lacked the personal emotional and spiritual
resources to be the mother her boys needed her to be. Par-
enting is a tremendously demanding responsibility. Raising
children in this world can be daunting at times. Where can
a parent turn for help?

The sad fact demonstrated by Susan's trial was that her
husband, David, numerous family members, relatives,
friends, teachers, former teachers, counselors, and neighbors all said they were available to help Susan at any time
she needed them. And yet Susan reported feeling intensely
"alone" with her life burdens with her children. She just
simply did not make use of the extensive social support
network she already had to assist her.

Here, mental health treatment would have helped Susan. Dr. Hammen, a research expert on depression, wrote that an individual's access to supports and resources may be important targets of treatment.[29]

Susan is learning to deal with the dark feelings inside her through Christian teachings regarding the sin nature. And she is learning a new way to approach God in confession of her failures promptly when she fails to live up to His moral standards. Pastor Long believes that justice was served by Susan's trial, and "Susan needed to face the responsibility for what she did."[30] In this sense, he believes that her trial "was necessary for Susan and for the community of Union."[31]

On October 25, 1994, Susan Smith did not know how to deal with the emotional pain of her past and of her immediate present. And there are times when everyone faces such overwhelming pain. You need only to listen to the lyrics of music on the radio to hear this theme. Some songs scream with deep hurt and disappointment. Some songs long for missing love.

In the past, Susan didn't know how to handle the stresses that built up over time. As an adult, she developed a lifestyle of infidelity, which generated her own keen stress, pressure, and embarrassment.[32] Research studies have shown that depressed women often contribute to the actual occurrence of negative events for themselves. Dr. Constance Hammen of the U.C.L.A. Psychology Department summarized her research findings when she wrote,

> Stress researchers have long emphasized one direction of causality—from events to symptoms—but I argue that it is essential also to consider the other direction: people contributing to events. Given that affective disorders are recurring and that they take a toll on people around them, such as marital

partners and children . . . some individuals have the
potential for getting caught up in a vicious cycle of
illness and events.[33]

Thus, instead of merely responding with depression to
difficult circumstances, these women generate their own
stress and then get depressed over it. Dr. Hammen's research found that 59 percent of the stress that "unipolar"
depresssed women (as Susan Smith was diagnosed by Dr.
Halleck) must cope with was "due at least in part to their
own behaviors or characteristics."[34]

This means that the depressed person is typically not
simply a victim of the stress around them, but that they
have characteristics which generate a majority of the stress
they experience in the first place. If such a person is a victim of stress, they themselves are, more likely than not,
their own primary victimizer.

The Rev. Long observes that Susan still has considerable depression. But as he ministers to her, he hopes to
help her realize that she could have thirty years in prison
to grow in faith, to share that faith with others, and
thereby have a meaningful existence.[35]

Currently, the Chaplain of the all-women's Columbia
College, Toni L. White, is ministering to Susan on a weekly
basis to promote her spiritual development and personal
adjustment. There are many aspects to Susan's broken life
that require understanding and healing, and if her spiritual
transformation has, in truth, begun with her Christian conversion, she will need to grow in her faith and spiritual
understanding to face the difficult issues of resolving all
the conflicts she has accumulated in her brief twenty-
three years of existence.

If Susan has taken a first step toward dealing with the
pain of her past by receiving God's forgiveness,[36] then

psychologically, that step can provide a basis for learning to forgive herself as well.[37]

In a letter to the editor of a national magazine, a reader wrote, "Her doctors have searched for a combination of drugs to stabilize her precarious mental condition? Where I live, her mental condition is called guilt, and no pills can take that away."[38] It is true that psychiatric treatment is no substitute for spiritual healing, but there is still a valid role for psychiatric and psychological treatment for Susan's intermittent depression.[39]

With her family tree containing so much depression among her relatives,[40] Susan needs to continue receiving ongoing psychiatric evaluations for monitoring her need for antidepressant medication and psychotherapy. Seymour Halleck, M.D., and Donald Morgan, M.D., testified in her trial that since imprisoned, Susan has been receiving Prozac.[41] There has been evidence that this medication is helping to alleviate her depressed condition. One of the advantages of prison for her is state-paid psychiatric treatment and twenty-four-hour monitoring for any suicidal behavior. She is in an environment that should ensure that she receives the treatment she needs for her disorder of depression.

The healing of the families of Susan and David Smith began with the sad funeral for Michael and Alex held at the Buffalo United Methodist Church on at 2 p.m. on November 6, 1994. Because of the intense grief and the presence of the national media, it was "quite difficult" according to Pastor Long. The four ministers who participated in the service offered a sense of comfort to the family. It was a very sad but meaningful day.

Now each family member needs to identify his own circle of social, emotional, and spiritual support. Close family members, close friends, clergy, and professional counselors are available to help.

The community of Union has already begun its healing process after experiencing this high-profile tragedy, according to the Rev. Mark Long. Community leaders understand that cover-up, revenge, and hatred must be replaced with truth, justice, and compassion if lasting healing is to be found for the Union community. Active steps have been taken to restore unity to Union.

The community needed to uncover the whole truth about Susan, Alex and Michael Smith. What was Susan's mental state just prior to and at the time she killed her sons? Was she responsible for her actions at the time of the boys' tragic killing? Does she deserve punishment? The full answer to these questions surfaced clearly during the painful trial process.

Before the trial, some in the community prayed for a successfully negotiated plea bargain, to help the town and the families heal faster.

Pursuing a death penalty trial in July 1995 in the small, very close-knit community of Union, did bring up the emotion and pain that the community felt back in November 1994 when Susan confessed to her crime. The shock, the anger, and the bewilderment—all those emotions came flooding back to the residents who had given up vacation time to search for the missing little boys, only to hear of their mother's confession of cold-blooded murder.

But in the final analysis, having all the pertinent facts brought out in court paved the way for long-term healing in the community. It's like surgery. Sometimes you have to deliberately plan to suffer and bleed through a targeted operation in the short run, in order to gain a lifetime of better health.

It would not have been enough to have the matter tried only in the press. An advantage of the American system of justice is that witnesses must swear to tell the truth, the whole truth and nothing but the truth. This requirement provides a potentially higher standard of knowledge about people's actions that touch the lives of others. The trial produced its awkward and painful moments in its meticulous process, but with the magnitude of the crime in question, it was the best long-term solution.

The trial was the best course toward providing some sort of closure for all involved. The townspeople wondered about the motive of this women. Why did she do it? Was she insane? And the evidence came forward from the prosecution and the defense in order to get a clear and balanced view of what happened that bleak night in October.

If a plea bargain had canceled a full trial, the public might have been left in the dark about critical facts in the case. This vacuum could have led to competing rumors and could have created public controversy and lingering doubts, leaving the community unsettled for a longer period of time. For this reason, accurate media coverage also played a vital role in community healing by fairly and promptly communicating the facts to the public.

The threat of the death penalty inherent in the trial process forced out much truth about who Susan Smith was and what she did. If there had been a plea bargain instead of a trial, then we would not have learned the full truth of Beverly Russell's incestuous relationship, the truth about Susan's numerous adulterous affairs, and the truth about whether Susan was sane at the time of the crime and able to make voluntary choices when she released the car into the lake with her children in it. Without this truth, healing would have been more difficult because it would have been hindered by doubts, speculation, and confusion.

The community needs to continue to *pursue justice, not revenge.* Susan's confession uncomfortably forced the public to come to terms with the fact that a mother murdered her helpless little children. Some would point out that Susan was "playing God" to intend to solve her problems by snuffing out the lives of her little children, and by contemplating suicide herself, as she confessed to.

The eight months that elapsed between Susan's arrest and her trial gave the community time to think through some issues before coming to a final conclusion on several matters. Initially, many sought revenge. "Women like Susan are not human beings," some said. And "Even animals don't kill their own offspring," said others erroneously.

But community leaders—such as the town mayor, the county sheriff, and the clergy—have continued to guide a public dialogue to overcome any hurtful emotional reactions of revenge, racism, or hatred in response to Susan's horrific behavior.

There is a decided difference between bitter revenge and just punishment. It is essential for Union not to shift blame where blame does not belong. Those in Union—and especially for her close family and friends—will need to be reminded in coming months and years to avoid shifting blame to themselves with endless speculation about "what if I had only done so and so." After all, that seems to be the defense maneuver of Susan herself to try to make others feel guilty for what Susan had done wrong herself.

It was wrong for Susan to kill her children and then blame a member of another race for her crime. That's the sinister and manipulative blame-shifting technique of falsely playing the "victim role." Blame-shifting is as old as Adam blaming Eve and Eve blaming the serpent in the Garden of Eden. It was wrong then, and is still wrong today.

The court impartially determined the extent to which Susan was responsible for what she did. No one else is responsible for what she did. Susan has contributed to the healing process by clearly taking responsibility for her actions. Her minister reports that she has turned away from the "I'll be God" attitude that motivated the killing of her own children. This repentant action by Susan will go a long way toward community healing. It is difficult, awkward, and perhaps impossible for us to forgive someone who does not admit to doing wrong. To "forgive" them is taken as an insult, because they don't admit they did anything wrong in the first place.

But since Susan has admitted that she did the wrong thing, forgiveness becomes a distinct possibility if there is a solid basis for the forgiveness.

The Union Ministerial Association took the lead in opposing the death penalty for Susan, and the ministers largely feel that justice was served by the trial. The ministers have been preaching forgiveness to their congregations. The Ministerial Association also sponsored Monday evening worship services during the trial.

So the opinion of many in Union is that healing is occurring for the community, and the primary leaders of that healing are the pastors of the churches.

The community's leaders and the law enforcement officials have worked together to affirm human dignity— that human life should be properly respected and that human responsibility is affirmed. Consider the contrast between Susan's disregard for the preciousness of her sons' lives and the thousands of dollars the county paid for extra security to protect Susan's life during the court process. The court provides an opportunity for justice to be rendered instead of revenge for being betrayed, revenge for unjust losses, or revenge for inciting racial strife.

Each individual community member in Union needs to channel [his or her] energy toward *practicing compassion*. With time, the level of rage [has] settled down. There remains some animosity in the community against Susan. And some concern remains over her allegation that a black man was responsible for taking her car and children. But over time, many people have softened their initial outrage, and the editor of the *Union Daily Times* reported, "Racial relations at this point have been very good. They have been good through this whole ordeal. It has not been a racial situation, it was not, even though Susan had identified a so-called perpetrator of this crime. The black community here rallied around her in search of these children. They were the first to pass out leaflets. They were the first to try to bring in leads thinking it may have been a black person. So as far as the racial issue is concerned here, it has never been an issue."[42]

Sadly, and almost unbelievably, David Smith received hate mail from around the nation with this message: "If you had been a good husband and weren't out fornicating and stayed home with your wife, then your children wouldn't have been murdered. . . ."[43] Others would be quick to regret the lack of compassion of the person who would write such hurtful words to a profoundly hurting and deeply grieving father. Healing is needed for such people who author such poisonous letters.

The tradition of the town of Union, which was named for the historic cooperative unity of different religious faiths sharing the same church sanctuary, is to take positive steps to express caring compassion, depending upon the situation.

Community leaders need to affirm the preciousness of all children's lives and the preciousness of all people of all races. Others should help young parents with the stress of rearing preschool children in town.

Many should find more ways to express their care for one another on a regular basis.

Many are praying for David Smith, for Susan Smith, and for their immediate families and should continue to do so.

Still others need to find the basis for being willing to forgive Susan as she transitions to abandoning excuses and blaming others, in order to repudiate her terrible offenses of sheer evil.

The stigma of mental illness needs to be continually addressed in Union, because that stigma can be an impediment to a person like Susan seeking help when she needs it. Today, Union is better equipped to provide mental health services than it was several years ago because the Saluda Mental Health Service in Rock Hill now has a satellite office in Union.

The tragedy of the Smith boys has alerted Union to a degree of indifference in the population. It has pointed to a need to look at the welfare of the community's children and people who need help.

All these steps—uncovering the whole truth, seeking justice rather than revenge, and practicing compassion—are essential for Union and our nation to find lasting healing after this tragedy of murder, lying, and racial blame-shifting by Susan Smith.

Some helpful lessons can be learned from the tragic Smith case:

1) Parents should identify their social and emotional support network of close friends and family members. There is also preventive value to psychological care at crisis points in a person's life. Finding someone to listen while you talk it out is important. Catastrophic thinking can lead to catastrophic behavior if you do not use your social support net-

work. There is much good help available, and there are straightforward ways to acquire such help from friends, family, counseling centers, or religious leaders.

2) When one is experiencing marital problems, good professional marriage counseling can be very helpful. Many churches provide pre-marriage counseling for a couple. (Susan's current minister believes that she and David did not receive such counseling before their wedding at another church in Bogansville, South Carolina.)

3) When one files for divorce, it is better to take time to heal, rather than jumping prematurely into another relationship.

4) A trial is best conducted by a court and not by the press.

5) Living a life of habitual lying and manipulation can spin a web that becomes a trap. Lying eventually destroys the person and harms others.

6) A community needs to have sympathy for a person married to a spouse with mental illness. It has been reported that David Smith had to cope with rapid mood shifts by his wife, Susan. Such spouses need emotional support.

7) The community needs to affirm the precious value of every child's life.

Out of all tragedies, some good emerges. If others needing help can be reached because of the Susan Smith tragedy, if just one murder or suicide can be prevented, then the community of Union, South Carolina, or perhaps other towns and cities across American, can say that a positive experience resulted from what appears to be a senseless act. The story of Susan's life behind bars has yet to unfold. Can her conversion and new psychological insights allow her to reach out to other inmates? Can she achieve some good in her life during the many years of her punishment? And will a mature woman over fifty years old come out of prison and have a place in society? These questions and others are yet to be answered. Now, the tragedy is over. Her life and perhaps ours will begin again.

Notes

INTRODUCTION

1. Professor Donald William Morgan is the director of the Forensic Psychiatry Training Program at the USC-affiliated teaching hospital, William S. Hall Psychiatric Institute. On July 10, 1995, Dr. Morgan testified in the court case, The State vs. Susan Vaughan Smith that he, Geoffrey McKee, Ph.D., forensic psychologist and Associate Professor, and Tracy Gunter-Justice, M.D., Forensic Psychiatry Fellow had jointly evaluated Susan Smith in response to the court order of March 23, 1995. Dr. Morgan testified that instead of the normal procedure of having the defendant in custody at the Hall Psychiatric Institute, he and his team of doctors were required to examine Susan Smith in prison at the Women's Correctional Facility. Dr. Morgan testified that he saw Susan five times for one and a half to two hours each time, and that both Dr. KcKee and Dr. Gunter accompanied him and took notes during the interviews. All three of the doctors participated in the interview process. Thus they interviewed her on April 20, 21, 24, May 5 and 12, and July 10, 1995. Dr. McKee also saw her for psychological testing for two sessions, Dr. Morgan testified.
2. When appropriate, I clarified to the representatives of the media that I was not one of the doctors who evaluated Susan Smith. Dr. Larry Faulkner (Director of the Hall Psychiatric Institute, Chairman of Neuropsychiatry and Behavioral Science, and Interim Dean of the USC School of Medicine) expressed his appreciation to me for serving the hospital and university in this way. Both Dr. Faulkner and Dr. McKee (the latter who was on the team of doctors who evaluated Susan Smith) personally told me that they appreciated my clarifications to the public, that I was not one of Susan Smith's doctors, and on this basis told me that they felt it was appropriate for me to write a book about Susan Smith that would

207

relate the public information from her trial to psychological research and theory. Because Susan Smith was never my patient, I offer my views not as her doctor, but as an educator in psychology. My theoretical interpretations should be taken in this context.

CHAPTER 1

1. Elizabeth Gleick, "Sex, Betrayal and Murder," *Time*, July 17, 1995, p. 33.
2. Lisa H. Towle, Investigative Reporter, *Time*, personal communication, June 29, 1995.
3. David Smith with Carol Calef, *Beyond All Reason: My Life with Susan Smith*. New York: Kensington Books, 1995.
4. Maria Eftimiades, *Sins of the Mother*. New York: St. Martin's Paperbacks, 1995, p. 45–46.
5. Elizabeth Gleick, "Sex, Betrayal and Murder," *Time*, July 17, 1995, p. 33.
6. Maria Eftimiades, *Sins of the Mother*. New York: St. Martin's Paperbacks, 1995, pp. 46–47.
7. David's perception of his marriage with Susan is revealed in his recent book, *Beyond All Reason: My Life with Susan Smith*. New York: Kensington, 1995.
8. Maria Eftimiades, *Sins of the Mother*. New York: St. Martin's Paperbacks, 1995, p. 56.
9. Elizabeth Gleick, "Sex, Betrayal and Murder," *Time*, July 17, 1995, p. 36.
10. From her written confession on November 3, 1994.
11. Anna Brown, "Prosecution rests case against Smith," *The Daily Times Union*, July 20, 1995, p. 1.

CHAPTER 2

1. According to the trial testimony of Seymour Halleck, M.D., who had conducted a psychiatric evaluation of Susan Vaughan Smith, which included review of the Vaughan family history information gathered by Arlene Andrew, Ph.D., a psychologist on the faculty of the University of South Carolina School of Social Work.
2. Dr. Seymour Halleck offered this testimony in Susan Smith's trial, and he clarified that these conclusions were based upon what Linda Vaughan Russell told him and what a counselor told him.
3. By Seymour Halleck, M.D., psychiatrist, on July 21, 1995.
4. Quotes from the testimony of Iris Rogers, currently a commercial account assistant in an insurance agency, in the Susan Smith trial on July 21, 1995.
5. Maria Eftimiades, *Sins of the Mother*. New York: St. Martin's Paperbacks, 1995, p. 34.
6. Dr. Seymour Halleck's courtroom testimony on July 21, 1995.
7. According to testimony by Susan's first cousin, Lee p. Harrison, on July 22, 1995, at Susan Smith's trial.

8. Sheriff Howard Wells read these details from the incident report in his testimony in the Susan Smith trial, on July 22, 1995.
9. Elizabeth Gleick, "Sex, Betrayal and Murder," *Time*, July 17, 1995, p. 32.
10. Ibid.
11. E. Mavis Hetherington, "Effects of father absence on personality development in adolescent daughters," *Developmental Psychology*, 1972, volume 7, pp. 313–326.
12. Testimony of Deborah Green at Susan Smith's trial on July 21, 1995.
13. Ibid.
14. Ibid.
15. David Smith with Carol Calef, *Beyond All Reason: My Life with Susan Smith*. New York: Kensington Books, 1995, p. 33–34.
16. David Smith with Carol Calef, *Beyond All Reason: My Life with Susan Smith*. New York: Kensington Books, 1995, pp. 34–35.
17. Maria Eftimiades, *Sins of the Mother*. New York: St. Martin's Paperbacks, 1995, p. 38.
18. David Smith with Carol Calef, *Beyond All Reason: My Life with Susan Smith*. New York: Kensington Books, 1995, pp. 49–50.
19. Described in Dr. Halleck's testimony on July 21, 1995 in Susan Smith's trial.
20. ". . . the trauma of losing a parent through death, divorce, or neglect shatters people's feelings of security, adequacy, and worth and leaves psychological scars that never completely heal. When children perceive themselves to be abandoned, feelings of inadequacy and self-devaluation develop. While the effect of abandonment varies. . . many children experiencing loss of a parent show disruption in normal personality development. The extent and impact of early childhood separation of the offender from a loved one may be a causative factor in violent offenses, including murder, rape, and assault" (p. 57). These are the conclusions of a study by Faith H. Leibman, "Childhood abandonment/adult rage: The root of violent criminal acts," *American Journal of Forensic Psychology*, 1992, volume 10, number 4, pp. 57–64.
21. G. R. Elliott, & C. Eisdorfer (editors), *Stress and Human Health: A Study by the Institute of Medicine, National Academy of Sciences*. New York: Springer, 1982; Kathleen Kim, & Selby Jacobs, "Stress of bereavement and consequent psychiatric illness," Chapter 7 in Carolyn M. Mazure (editor), *Does Stress Cause Psychiatric Illness?* Washington, DC: American Psychiatric Press, 1995, pp. 187–219.
22. R. H. Holmes, & R. H. Rahe, "The social readjustment rating scale," *Journal of Psychosomatic Research*, 1967, volume 11, pp. 213–218.
23. J. Birtchnell, "The relationship between attempted suicide, depression, and parent death," *British Journal of Psychiatry*, 1970, volume 116, pp. 307–313.
24. G. E. Murphy, M. D. Armstrong, S. L. Heremele, et al, "Suicide and alcoholism, *Archives of General Psychiatry*, 1979, volume 36, pp. 65–69.
25. In testimony given on July 21, 1995.
26. Clif LeBlanc, Margaret N. O'Shea, and Twila Decker, "2 Sides Spar over Smith's Psyche," *The State*, July 19, 1995, p. A6.

CHAPTER 3

1. Margaret N. O'Shea, Clif LeBlanc, & Twila Decker, "'I failed'" Stepfather faces Jury," *The State*, July 28, 1995, p. A1.
2. Ibid.
3. Robert Davis, "Stepfather pleads for Smith's life," *USA Today*, July 28, 1995, p. 3A.
4. Elizabeth Gleick, "Sex, Betrayal and Murder," *Time*, July 17, 1995, p. 32.
5. Twila Decker, "Records: Stepfather fondled Smith/Complaints detail repeated incidents. *The State*, April 12, 1995, p. A1; Elizabeth Gleick, "Sex, Betrayal and Murder," *Time*, July 17, 1995, p. 32.
6. Ibid.
7. Ibid.
8. Marc Peyser & Ginny Carroll, "Southern Gothic on Trial, Susan Smith: Will the child-killer be put to death?" *Newsweek*, July 17, 1995, p. 29.
9. Ibid.
10. Courtroom testimony by Seymour Halleck, M.D., professor of psychiatry, University of North Carolina, Chapel Hill, in the double murder trial of Susan V. Smith on July 21, 1995, based upon his evaluation of her in 1995 while in prison, for the defense attorneys.
11. Ibid.
12. Ibid.
13. Ibid.
14. Maria Eftimiades, *Sins of the Mother*. New York: St Martin's Paperbacks, 1995, p. 37.
15. Ibid.
16. According to research by Delia Esparza, "Maternal support and stress response in sexually abused girls," *Issues in Mental Health Nursing*, 1993, volume 14, pp. 85–107.
17. Twila Decker, "Records: Stepfather fondled Smith/Complaints detail repeated incidents," *The State*, April 12, 1995, p. A1.
18. Ibid.
19. Elizabeth Gleick, "Sex, Betrayal and Murder," *Time*, July 17, 1995, pp. 32–33.
20. Margaret N. O'Shea, Clif LeBlanc, & Twila Decker, "'I failed'" Stepfather faces Jury," *The State*, July 28, 1995, p. A1.
21. Elizabeth Gleick, "Sex, Betrayal and Murder," *Time*, July 17, 1995, p. 33.
22. Christopher Bagley, "Early Sexual Experience and Sexual Victimization of Children and Adolescents," Chapter 7 in George A. Rekers (Editor), *Handbook of Child and Adolescent Sexual Problems*. New York: Lexington Books of The Free Press/Simon & Schuster, 1995.
23. Ibid., pp. 135–163.
24. Ibid.
25. Ibid.
26. Ibid.
27. Benjamin B. Wolman (editor), *Dictionary of Behavioral Science*. New York: Van Nostrand Reinhold Company, 1973, p. 103.
28. Ibid.

29. Courtroom testimony by Seymour Halleck, M.D., professor of psychiatry, University of North Carolina, Chapel Hill, in the double murder trial of Susan V. Smith on July 21, 1995.
30. Ibid.
31. Ibid.
32. Ibid.
33. Margaret N. O'Shea, "Cops doubted story, but truth shocked them." *The State*, July 21, 1995, p. A8.
34. Ibid.
35. George A. Rekers (editor), *Handbook of Child and Adolescent Sexual Problems*. New York: Lexington Books of The Free Press/Simon & Schuster, 1995, p. 209.

CHAPTER 4

1. David Smith with Carol Calef, *Beyond All Reason: My Life with Susan Smith*. New York: Kensington Books, 1995, p. 35.
2. Ibid.
3. David Smith with Carol Calef, *Beyond All Reason: My Life with Susan Smith*. New York: Kensington Books, 1995, p. 36.
4. Sexualized dating by adolescents is associated with psychological risks of interpersonal conflicts, emotional conflicts, internalized guilt over the transgression of moral standards for sexual conduct, and provides a false psychological sense of emotional intimacy which is disruptive to the adolescent's psychological development. See the psychological literature on this reviewed by George A. Rekers and Richard C. Hohn, "Sex education should exclusively endorse abstinence as the only effective prevention of the unacceptable risks of nonmarital sexual relations," Chapter 8 in James T. Sears and James Carper (Editors), *Public Education and Religion: Conversations for an Enlarging Public Square*. New York: Teachers College Press, 1996, in press.
5. Based upon Susan Brown's testimony at Susan Smith's trial on July 19, 1995.
6. Ibid.
7. Ibid.
8. Ibid.
9. According to Sandy Williams' sworn testimony in Susan Smith's trial on July 19, 1995.
10. Dialogue extrapolated from the courtroom testimony of Tom Findlay at the Susan Smith trial on July 19, 1995.
11. Marc Peyser & Ginny Carroll, "Southern Gothic on Trial, Susan Smith: Will the child-killer be put to death?" *Newsweek*, July 17, 1995, p. 29.

CHAPTER 5

1. As reprinted in the Spartanburg *Herald-Journal*, July 20, 1995, p. A13.
2. Margaret N. O'Shea, Clif LeBlanc, and Twila Decker, "Jurors join dad's tears for lost boys," *The State*, July 26, 1995, p. A6.

3. Ibid.
4. As quoted by Margaret N. O'Shea, Clif LeBlanc, Twila Decker, Nina Brook, & Doug Nye, "Ex-husband says Smith deserves no 2nd chance," *The State*, July 26, 1995, p. A6.
5. Dr. Donald Morgan also testified on July 10, 1995, that in his view Susan V. Smith was criminally responsible at the time of the crime. He did a separate evaluation to determine that Susan had the capacity to conform, to know right from wrong.
6. American Psychological Association, *Diagnostic and Statistical Manual of Mental Disorders, Fourth Edition.* Washington, D.C.: American Psychological Association, 1994.
7. Testimony by Donald Morgan, M.D., D.Sc., in Susan Smith's trial on July 10, 1995. Dr. Morgan testified that Susan had an Adjustment Disorder with Mixed Emotional Features at the time of the crime she was charged with, and that she had Major Depression at the time of the evaluation while she was awaiting trial.
8. A. H. Loewy, *Criminal law.* St. Paul, MN: West, 1975.
9. G. B. Melton, J. Petrila, N. G. Poythress, & C. Slobogin, *Psychological evaluations for the courts.* New York: Guilford, 1987.
10. Act No. 323, 1, 1988.
11. Act No. 323, 2, 1988.
12. S.C. Supreme Court, 1992, p. 44.
13. Geoffrey R. McKee, "Insanity and adultery: Forensic implications of a divorce case," *Psychological Reports*, 1995, volume 76, pp. 427–434.
14. Geoffrey R. McKee, "Insanity and adultery: Forensic implications of a divorce case," *Psychological Reports*, 1995, volume 76, p. 430.
15. The defense strategy described by Robert Davis, "Smith defense courting sympathy," *USA Today*, July 21, 1995, p. 3A.
16. See summary by Robert Davis, "Smith defense courting sympathy," *USA Today*, July 21, 1995, p. 3A.

CHAPTER 6

1. According to the courtroom testimony at Susan Smith's trial by her defense psychiatrist, Seymour Halleck, M.D., July 21, 1995.
2. Courtroom testimony by Shirley McCloud in Susan Smith Trial, July 18, 1995; and Maria Eftimiades, *Sins of the Mother.* New York: St Martin's Paperbacks, 1995, p. 10.
3. Ibid.
4. Ibid.
5. David Smith with Carol Calef, *Beyond All Reason: My Life with Susan Smith.* New York: Kensington Books, 1995, p. 4.
6. Gary Henderson, Nine Days in Union: The Search for Alex and Michael Smith. Spartanburg, SC: Honoribus Press, 1995.
7. Testimony by Tom Findlay at Susan Smith's trial on July 19, 1995.
8. Ibid.

9. Testimony by Susan Brown at Susan Smith's trial on July 19, 1995.
10. Gary Henderson, *Nine Days in Union: The Search for Alex and Michael Smith*. Spartanburg, SC: Honoribus Press, 1995, p. 18.
11. Ibid., p. 22.
12. Ibid., p. 7.
13. Ibid., p. 25.
14. David Smith with Carol Calef, *Beyond All Reason: My Life with Susan Smith*. New York: Kensington Books, 1995, p. 64.
15. Testimony of David A. Caldwell of SLED at Susan Smith's trial, on July 19, 1995.
16. Ibid.
17. Ibid.
18. David Smith with Carol Calef, *Beyond All Reason: My Life with Susan Smith*. New York: Kensington Books, 1995, pp. 64–65.
19. Testimony of David A. Caldwell of SLED at Susan Smith's trial, on July 19, 1995.
20. Testimony by David Allen Espie, III, FBI agent, at the trial of Susan Smith, on July 19, 1995.
21. Ibid.
22. Ibid.
23. Ibid.
24. Ibid.
25. Gary Henderson, *Nine Days in Union: The Search for Alex and Michael Smith*. Spartanburg, SC: Honoribus Press, 1995, p. 33.
26. Margaret N. O'Shea, "Cops doubted story, but truth shocked them," *The State Extra*, July 21, 1995, Internet story, p. 1.
27. Margaret N. O'Shea, Clif LeBlanc, & Twila Decker, "Penalty phase focuses on Smith's lies," *The State*, July 25, 1995, p. A7.

CHAPTER 7

1. Testimony by SLED Agent James Logan at Susan Smith's trial, on July 20, 1995.
2. Ibid.
3. Ibid.
4. Ibid.
5. Ibid.
6. These factors influencing Susan to be ready to confess were identified by Susan's defense attorney's co-counsel, Judy Clarke, in her remarks to Judge William Howard at the pretrial hearing on admissibility of Susan's confession, at the court hearing on July 17, 1995.
7. Testimony by Sheriff Howard Wells at the pretrial court hearing for the Susan Smith trial, on July 17, 1995.
8. Testimony of Sheriff Howard Wells in Susan Smith's trial, on July 22, 1995.
9. According to testimony by FBIagent Carol Allison at Susan Smith's trial, July 17, 1995.

10. Ibid.

11. David Smith with Carol Calef, *Beyond All Reason: My Life with Susan Smith*. New York: Kensington Books, 1995, p. vii.

12. Testimony in the Susan Smith trial on July 25, 1995, as quoted by Margaret N. O'Shea, Clif LeBlanc, and Twila Decker, "Jurors join dad's tears for lost boys," *The State*, July 26, 1995, p. A1.

13. Ibid.

14. "Parents who murder," *Atlanta Constitution*, July 29, 1995.

15. Margaret N. O'Shea, Clif LeBlanc, & Twila Decker, "Penalty phase focuses on Smith's lies," *The State*, July 25, 1995, p. A7.

16. As quoted by Clif LeBlanc and Twila Decker, "Pastors preach forgiveness: As trial begins, Union ministers call for mercy," *The State*, July 10, 1995, p. A7.

17. Barbara Walters with David Smith on the "20/20" television program broadcast on July 28, 1995.

CHAPTER 8

1. Testimony of Tom Findlay at Susan Smith's trial on July 19, 1995.

2. Marc Peyser & Ginny Carroll, "Southern Gothic on Trial, Susan Smith: Will the child-killer be put to death?" *Newsweek*, July 17, 1995, p. 29.

3. In addition to examining Susan Smith's words, her handwriting has also been analyzed by a leading graphology expert, Charles Hamilton. Hamilton was asked on an ABC national news broadcast to comment on his analysis of her handwriting in her confession. Hamilton concluded that Susan's handwriting shows she has a "secretive personality," with "emotional instability . . . with rampant emotions." The heavy pressure of her handwriting was interpreted as showing "brutality and aggression." Other features of her handwriting suggested "a neurotic, unbalanced and dangerously unsocial character." He noted indicators of "insincerity," "confusion," "pessimism," "insecurity," and "indecision."

4 Maria Eftimiades, *Sins of the Mother*. New York: St. Martin's Paperbacks, 1995, p. 184.

5. Ibid.

6. Dominique Bourget, and John M. W. Bradford, "Homicidal parents," *Canadian Journal of Psychiatry*, April 1990, volume 35, pp. 233–237; F. J. Arboleda and A. Power, "The Medea syndrome," *American Journal of Forensic Psychiatry*, 1983, volume 4, number 2, pp. 61–66; P. T. D'Orban, "Female homicide, *Irish Journal of Psychological Medicine*, 1990, volume 7, number 1, pp. 64–70; S. J. Shea, G. R. McKee, A. M. Foster, and C. Bostdorff, "Characteristics of women who kill their children," paper presented to the Annual Convention of the American Psychological Association, August 13, 1995.

7. Eighteen thousand children annually are permanently disabled by severe physical abuse and another 142,000 are seriously injured by abuse annually in the United States. Domestic abuse is reported to be strongly associated to the child abuse cases that end in death of the child. These

findings were reported by the study commissioned by the U.S. Advisory Board on Child Abuse and Neglect, *A Nation's Shame: Fatal Child Abuse and Neglect in the United States,* a federal report presented to the U.S. Congress and the White House in Spring 1995. See also the related study by A. S. Husain & A. Daniel, "A comparative study of filicidal and abusive mothers," *Canadian Journal of Psychiatry,* November 1984, volume 29, number 7, pp. 596–598.

8. One study found the killing of the child was done in "a rage of impatience and anger" and was a result of "beating or shaking," reported by Ann Goetting, "When parents kill their young children," *Journal of Family Violence,* December 1988, volume 3, number 4, pp. 339–346; An overview of research and public policy on this problem is presented by Frank Cavalier, "Parents killing kids: a nation's shame," *American Psychological Association Monitor,* August 1995, volume 26, number 8, p. 34; Cavalier reported on the study commissioned by the U.S. Advisory Board on Child Abuse and Neglect, *A Nation's Shame: Fatal Child Abuse and Neglect in the United States,* a federal report presented to the U.S. Congress and the White House in Spring 1995. The federal report may be obtained from the board at (800) 394–3366 or (703) 385–7565. See also M. Newlands and J. S. Emery, "Child abuse and cot deaths," *Child Abuse and Neglect,* 1991, volume 15, number 3, pp. 275–278. S. deSilva, & R. K. Oates, "Child homicide: the extreme of child abuse," *The Medical Journal of Australia,* vol. 158, No. 1, pp 300–301.

9. E. Cherland and P. C. Matthews, "Attempted murder of a newborn," *Canadian Journal of Psychiatry,* May 1989, volume 34, number 4, pp. 337–339; J. Bieder, "The case history of a child-murderer," *Annales Medico Psychologiques,* 1978, volume 136, number 1, pp. 184–190; J. K. Amighi, "Some thoughts on the cross-cultural study of maternal warmth and detachment," *Pre- and Peri-Natal Psychology Journal,* 1990, volume 5, number 2, pp. 131–146.

10. P. J. Resnick, "Child murder by parents: a psychiatric review of filicide," *American Journal of Psychiatry,* 1969, volume 126, number 3, pp. 325–334.

11. These parents kill their children while they are out of contact with reality while in a psychotic state. See Dominique Bourget and John M. Bradford, "Affective disorder and homicide," *Canadian Journal of Psychiatry,* April 1987, volume 32, number 3, 222–225; A. S. Husain, & A. Daniel, "A comparative study of filicidal and abusive mothers," *Canadian Journal of Psychiatry,* November 1984, volume 29, number 7, pp. 596–598; L. Lidberg, I. M. Winborg, and M. Asberg, "Low cerebrospinal fluid levels of 5-hydroxyindoleacetic acid and murder-suicide," *Nordic Journal of Psychiatry,* 1992, volume 46, number 6, pp. 419–420; Dominique Bourget and Alain Labelle, "Homicide, infanticide, and filicide," *Psychiatric Clinics of North America,* September 1992, volume 15, number 3, pp. 661–673.

12. C. E. Banzato, "Depressao y filicidio (Depression and felicide)," *Jornal Brasileiro de Psiquiatria,* 1990, volume 39, number 6, 301–306.

13. Dominique Bourget, and John M. W. Bradford, "Homicidal parents," *Canadian Journal of Psychiatry*, April 1990, Volume 35, pp. 233–237. There is a parallel in cases in which fathers "sacrifice" a child by murder to manipulate dynamics with the mother; see Jean Cordier, "L'enfant, victime privilegiee du drame passionnell ("The child, privileged victim of crimes of passion"), *Victimology*, 1983, volume 8, numbers 1–2, pp. 131–136. J. M. Dawson, & P. A. Langan, *Murder in Families*. Bureau of Justice Statistics, Special Report, July 1994. Washington, D.C.: Bureau of Justice Statistics.

14. In a study of women forensically evaluated for murder or attempted murder of their biological children, the victims tended to be male and the filicides (murder of one's children) "were motivated by revenge; the mother's anger toward the child's father was displaced onto the male child, often the youngest, who reminded the mother of the child's father"; Marsha J. Lomis, "Maternal filicide," *International Journal of Law and Psychiatry*, 1986, volume 9, number 4, 503–506.

15. Clif LeBlanc, Margaret N. O'Shea, and Twila Decker, "2 Sides Spar over Smith's Psyche," *The State*, July 19, 1995, p. A1.

16. Summary of testimony of witnesses on July 19, 1995, Anna Brown, "Prosecution rests case against Smith," *The Daily Times Union*, July 20, 1995, p. 1.

17. Anna Brown, "Prosecution rests case against Smith," *The Daily Times Union*, July 20, 1995, p. 1.

18. As quoted by Clif LeBlanc, Margaret N. O'Shea, and Twila Decker, "2 Sides Spar over Smith's Psyche," *The State*, July 19, 1995, p. A6.

19. Ibid.

20. Ibid.

CHAPTER 9

1. Marc Peyser & Ginny Carroll, "Southern Gothic on Trial, Susan Smith: Will the child-killer be put to death?" *Newsweek*, July 17, 1995, p. 29.

2. As quoted by Clif LeBlanc and Twila Decker, "Pastors preach forgiveness: As trial begins, Union ministers call for mercy," *The State*, July 10, 1995, p. A7.

3. In the Newsweek Poll that sampled the general United States population, 63% said they favor the death penalty for Susan Smith and 28% were opposed. See Tom Morganthau, Vern E. Smith, Margaret O'Shea, & Ginny Carroll, "Condemned to Life," *Newsweek*, August 7, 1995, p. 20.

4. Elizabeth Landt, "Union County Courthouse," *The State*, July 10, 1995, p. A7.

5. Ibid.

6. "Mail," *People*, July 31, 1995, p. 4.

7. Letter by Barbara T. Wilder, *People*, July 31, 1995, p. 4.

8. Testimony of Seymour Hallek, M.D., in the Susan Smith trial, on July 21, 1995.

9. CNN "TalkBack Live" with Susan Rook, on January 16, 1995.

10. Ibid.
11. Ibid.
12. "Women who kill usually escape ultimate penalty," *Atlanta Constitution*, July 29, 1995.
13. According to Watt Espy, quoted in "Women who kill usually escape ultimate penalty," *Atlanta Constitution*, July 29, 1995.
14. CNN TalkBack Live broadcasts on punishment for Susan Smith, July 18, 1995, and on forgiveness of Susan Smith, July 21; see also Marc Peyser & Ginny Carroll, "Southern Gothic on Trial, Susan Smith: Will the child-killer be put to death?" *Newsweek*, July 17, 1995, p. 29.
15. David Smith with Carol Calef, *Beyond All Reason: My Life with Susan Smith*. New York: Kensington Books, 1995, p. vii–viii.

CHAPTER 10

1. Dramatic personality reorganization with major positive shifts in behavior and mental states have been reported with Christian conversion. It has been suggested that conversion experiences should be more closely studied by the psychological and behavioral sciences because the potency of conversion compared with psychotherapy's potency "looks like atomic power compared with dynamite" as Bergin (1983) quoted Marks (1978). See I. M. Marks., "Behavioral psychotherapy of adult neurosis," in S. L. Garfield and A. E. Bergin (Editors), *Handbook of Psychotherapy and Behavior Change, Second Edition*. New York: Wiley, 1978; and Allen E. Bergin, "Religiosity and Mental Health: A Critical Reevaluation and Meta-Analysis," *Professional Psychology: Research and Practice*, 1983, volume 14, number 2, pp. 170–184.
2. Testimony of Seymour Halleck, M.D., at Susan Smith's trial, on July 21, 1995.
3. Clif LeBlanc and Twila Decker, "Pastors preach forgiveness," *The State*, July 10, 1995, p. A1.
4. The quotes of these three pastors are from Clif LeBlanc and Twila Decker, "Pastors preach forgiveness," *The State*, July 10, 1995, p. A1.
5. Gary Henderson, "Yellow ribbons fly for Union children," *Herald-Journal*, October 28, 1994, p. A1.
6. Quote from interview with the Rev. Mark Long, Pastor of the Buffalo United Methodist Church of Union, South Carolina, on August 7, 1995.
7. See for example, Michael Argyle, "The psychological explanation of religious experience," *Psyke and Logos*, 1990, volume 11, number 2, pp. 267–274.
8. Quote from interview with the Rev. Mark Long, Pastor of the Buffalo United Methodist Church of Union, South Carolina, on August 7, 1995.
9. For a basis of this form of pastoral counseling, see Walter J. Koehler, *Counseling and Confession: The Role of Confession and Absolution in Pastoral Counseling*. St Louis: Concordia Publishing House, 1982; see also Earl D. Wilson, *Counseling and Guilt*. Waco, TX: Word Books, 1987.

10. "Relationships may be crucial to the conversion process in a variety of ways," writes Lewis R. Rambo in *Understanding Religious Conversion*. New Haven: Yale University Press, 1993, p. 108 (see pp. 108 to 133 for a review of the psychology of relationships in conversions).

11. Clif LeBlanc and Twila Decker, "Pastors preach forgiveness: As trial begins, Union ministers call for mercy," *The State*, July 10, 1995, p. A7.

12. See examples of prison conversions in James Craig Holte, *The Conversion Experience in America: A Sourcebook on Religious Conversion Autobiography*. New York: Greenwood Press, 1992.

13. See, for example, David Belgum, *Guilt: Where Religion and Psychology Meet*. Minneapolis, MN: Augsburg Publishing House, 1963; Peter Homans (Editor), *The Dialogue Between Theology and Psychology*. Chicago: The University of Chicago Press, 1968.

14. See the translation of spiritual experiences such as Christian conversion and experiences of God and others in Oxford University (England) affiliated Michael Argyle, "The psychological explanation of religious experience," *Psyke and Logos*, 1990, volume 11, number 2, pp. 267–274.

15. Susan's life story and recent claim to Christian conversion could be studied within the theoretical context of the stages of faith development as described by James W. Fowler, *Stages of Faith: The Psychology of Human Development and the Quest for Meaning*. San Francisco, CA: Harper & Row, 1981; see also Kenneth Stokes (Editor), *Faith Development in the Adult Life Cycle*. New York: W. H. Sadlier, Inc., 1982.

16. The relationship between an individual's childhood relationships with parental figures and their subsequent religious involvements and Christian conversion experiences is the subject of the research reported by the University of South Carolina's Lee A. Kirkpatrick and Phillip R. Shaver, "Attachment theory and religion: Childhood attachments, religious beliefs, and conversion," *Journal for the Scientific Study of Religion*, September 1990, volume 29, number 3, pp. 315–334.

17. See Peter Homans (Editor), *The Dialogue Between Theology and Psychology*. Chicago: The University of Chicago Press, 1968.

18. See the discussion of psychospiritual problems and conversion to a new faith in David Lukoff, Francis Lu, and Robert Turner, "Toward a more culturally sensitive DSM-IV: Psychoreligious and psychospiritual problems," *Journal of Nervous and Mental Disease*, November 1992, volume 180, number 11, pp. 673–682.

19. This section is a theoretical synthesis of the individual pieces of data from Susan Smith's trial and what her pastor, Mark Long, told me by interview, placed with a process model to explain conversion as a process that is facilitated through the cognitive states of the individual. In this context, see the model of religious conversion presented by Emory University's John E. Pitt, "Why people convert: A balance theoretical approach to religious conversion," *Pastoral Psychology*, January 1991, volume 39, number 3, pp. 171–183.

20. According to a survey of the United States population, 61% of women and 59% of men believe in the existence of hell. 3% of women and 5% of

men believe that they have an "excellent or good chance of going to hell." 3% of church attenders and 7% of nonmembers of churches also believe that they have an "excellent or good chance of going to hell." See Jeffery L. Sheler, "Hell's sober comeback," *U.S. News & World Report*, March 25, 1991, pp. 56–64.

21. It is significant that Susan V. Smith's form of "intermittent depression," as psychiatrist Seymour Halleck diagnosed it, occurred only when Susan was alone. One might theorize that this was evidence that a core problem was a psychospiritual problem, in that if she had a close, personal relationship with God, she would never have experienced the sense of frightening and depressing isolation that she had when other human beings were not with her. If she had an assurance that God heard her prayers and interacted with her life, she could have been comforted by her prayerful conversations with God when other human beings were not around her. See the discussion of psychospiritual or psychoreligious problems and their relationship to the disorders listed in the *Diagnostic and Statistical Manual of Mental Disorders*, by David Lukoff, Francis Lu, and Robert Turner, "Toward a more culturally sensitive DSM-IV: Psychoreligious and psychospiritual problems," *Journal of Nervous and Mental Disease*, November 1992, volume 180, number 11, pp. 673–682.

22. From an interview with the Rev. Mark Long, Pastor of the Buffalo United Methodist Church of Union, South Carolina, on August 7, 1995.

23. See the empirical research on sudden versus gradual conscious decision to convert to Christianity by Stanford University affiliated Christine Liu, "Becoming a Christian consciously versus nonconsciously," *Journal of Psychology and Theology*, Winter 1991, volume 19, number 4, pp. 364–375.

24. See the discussion of the relationship between Christian conversion and various dimensions of pastoral care for a person facing death, by Harvard University's James L. Adams, "Palliative care in the light of early Christian concepts," *Journal of Palliative Care*, September 1989, volume 5, number 3, pp. 5–8.

25. Quote from the Rev. Mark Long by Jesse J. Holland (Associated Press Writer), "Ms. Smith ready to die, pastor says," *Union Daily Times*, July 10, 1995, p. 1.

26. Ibid.

27. Quoted by Clif LeBlanc & Twila Decker, "Pastors preach forgiveness," *The State*, July 10, 1995, p. A7.

28. Interview with the Rev. Mark Long, Pastor of the Buffalo United Methodist Church, Union, South Carolina, on August 7, 1995. According to a survey of the United States population, 81% of women and 74% of men believe in the existence of heaven. 81% of women and 73% of men believe that they have an "excellent or good chance of going to heaven." 83% of church attenders and 65% of nonmembers of churches also believe that they have an "excellent or good chance of going to heaven." See Jeffery L. Sheler, "Hell's sober comeback," *U.S. News & World Report*, March 25, 1991, pp. 56–64.

29. Constance L. Hammen, Ph.D., "Stress and the course of unipolar and bipolar disorders. Chapter 4 in Carolyn M. Mazure, *Does Stress Cause*

Psychiatric Illness? Washington, DC: American Psychiatric Press, 1995, p. 107.

30. Interview with the Rev. Mark Long, Pastor of the Buffalo United Methodist Church, Union, South Carolina, on August 7, 1995.

31. Ibid.

32. See the research of Constance L. Hammen, Ph.D., "Stress and the course of unipolar and bipolar disorders. Chapter 4 in Carolyn M. Mazure, *Does Stress Cause Psychiatric Illness?* Washington, DC: American Psychiatric Press, 1995, pp. 87–110.

33. Constance L. Hammen, Ph.D., "Stress and the course of unipolar and bipolar disorders. Chapter 4 in Carolyn M. Mazure, *Does Stress Cause Psychiatric Illness?* Washington, DC: American Psychiatric Press, 1995, p. 101.

34. Constance L. Hammen, Ph.D., "Stress and the course of unipolar and bipolar disorders. Chapter 4 in Carolyn M. Mazure, *Does Stress Cause Psychiatric Illness?* Washington, DC: American Psychiatric Press, 1995, p. 102.

35. Pastor Long will be involved in helping Susan develop new hope for living. See Hendrika VandeKempe, "Hope in psychotherapy," *Journal of Psychology and Christianity*, 1984, volume 3, number 1, pp. 27–35; some empirical research demonstrates the connection between optimism in life and form of religiosity—see S. Sethi and M. E. P. Seligman, "Optimism and fundamentalism," *Psychological Science*, July 1993, volume 4, number 4, pp. 256–259.

36. See the discussion of psychospiritual or psychoreligious problems and their relationship to the disorders listed in the *Diagnostic and Statistical Manual of Mental Disorders*, by David Lukoff, Francis Lu, and Robert Turner, "Toward a more culturally sensitive DSM-IV: Psychoreligious and psychospiritual problems," *Journal of Nervous and Mental Disease*, November 1992, volume 180, number 11, pp. 673–682; see also a discussion of theistic realism as an alternative viewpoint for conducting psychotherapy by Allen E. Bergin, "Psychotherapy and religious values," *Journal of Consulting and Clinical Psychology*, 1980, volume 48, number 1, pp. 95–105; see Lewis R. Rambo, *Understanding Religious Conversion*. New Haven: Yale University Press, 1993.

37. In a meta-analysis of the empirical research on the relationship between religiosity and mental health, no support was found for the preconception that spirituality or religiosity is correlated with psychopathology, but instead a slightly positive correlation was found between mental health and religiosity. See Allen E. Bergin, "Religiosity and mental Health: A critical reevaluation and meta-analysis," *Professional Psychology: Research and Practice*, 1983, volume 14, number 2, pp. 170–184. See also Florence A. Summerin, *Religion and Mental Health: A Bibliography*. National Institute of Mental Health, U.S. Department of Health and Human Services. Washington, D.C.: U.S. Government Printing Office, 1980, DHHS Publication No. (ADM) 80–964. Religious values of the therapist and of the patient have been found to be important variables in psychotherapy;

see Julie Giglio, "The impact of patients' and therapists' religious values on psychotherapy," *Hospital and Community Psychiatry*, August 1993, volume 44, number 8, pp. 768–711.

38. "Mail," *People*, July 31, 1995, p. 4.

39. Psychotherapy, psychiatric medication treatment, and spiritual ministry to a person have interrelationships which can be complementary and which can be integrated. See Lillian H. Robinson (Editor), *Psychiatry and Religion: Overlapping Concerns*. Washington, D.C.: American Psychiatric Press, 1986.

40. Dr. Donald Morgan concluded from his evaluation that Susan has a biological predisposition to depression, according to his testimony on July 10, 1995.

41. Testimony by Donald Morgan, M.D., D.Sc., in Susan Smith's trial on July 10, 1995.

42. Interview of Don Wilder on CNN's "TalkBack Live" with Susan Rook, January 16, 1994.

43. David Smith with Carol Calef, *Beyond All Reason: My Life with Susan Smith*. New York: Kensington Books, 1995, p. viii.

Glossary

Abandoned/unwanted child profile is one profile of parents who kill their child in which the parent (usually the mother) abandons her baby to die. These are often cases in which the mother is not married to the father of the child, and usually occurs shortly after the baby's birth.

"Abuse excuse" (a slang term used by the general public and the mass media) is the attempt to escape personal responsibility for one's actions by appealing to one's past experience of unjust abuse by another person.

Actus reus is a legal term for the capacity of a person to voluntarily perform an act. An individual's misconduct can be judged to be a crime only if he or she voluntarily performs a criminal act (*actus reus*) and has a guilty mind (*mens rea*) at the time of that act.

Adjustment Disorder is a diagnosis for an individual's difficulty in coping to his or her environmental situations, which results in a set of distressing emotions and/or problem behaviors that occur in response to an identifiable stressor. The reaction can cause significant impairment in social, school, or work functioning. The symptoms start within three months of the onset of the stressor. This diagnosis is listed in the *Diagnostic and Statistical Manual of Mental Disorders, Fourth Edition* (the standard handbook for psychiatrists, psychologists, physicians, and psychiatric social workers).

Alcoholism is the condition of being addicted to drinking alcohol, manifested by repeated drinking that injures one's health, one's finances, or one's relationships with others. The physical dependence on alcohol is evidenced by either developing a tolerance for it or the presence of withdrawal symptoms when alcohol intake is reduced or ceased. The individual with alcoholism feels compelled to drink alcohol as long as the alcohol is available, and does not regularly abstain from drinking alcohol unless kept from alcohol by the environment. Psychological dependence on alcohol is also present, and the person has impaired job performance.

Ambivalence is the condition of having mixed feelings or a feeling of confusion that accompanies having contradictory thoughts, attitudes, desires, or emotions toward a specific person, situation, or object. A person who feels ambivalent will often have both positive and negative feelings about something or someone. Some ambivalence is experienced by normally adjusted people, but in a strong form, ambivalence is typically an indicator of a mental disorder.

Anoxia is a medical condition of having insufficient oxygen, which can alter mental states due to oxygen deficiency for normal brain functioning. There is a number of different types of anoxia, classified according to the cause of the lack of oxygen.

Anxiety is increased tension, apprehension, or uneasiness from anticipating a danger or negative experience. The emotion mainly originates from within the person's own mind. The person typically is not aware or does not recognize the source of this emotion, unlike *fear* which is the emotion in response usually to a consciously recognized external danger.

Atypical means abnormal.

Bereavement is feeling grief, feeling desolate, or feeling deprived after the loss of a loved one.

Bipolar disorder is a diagnosis listed in the *Diagnostic and Statistical Manual of Mental Disorders, Fourth Edition,* which refers to a mood disorder in which the individual experiences episodes of both depression and mania. Depression is characterized by lowered mood, whereas mania is characterized by excitement, expansive, euphoric, or irritable mood, with hyperactivity, decreased need for sleep, distractibility, impaired judgment, pressured speech, and flight of ideas (sometimes with delusions). This disorder was previously named, "manic-depressive illness."

Borderline personality disorder is a diagnosis listed in the *Diagnostic and Statistical Manual of mental Disorders, Fourth Edition,* which refers to a condition of having a long-standing pattern of instability in emotions, in self-image, and in relating to others, together with a pronounced impulsiveness which begins in early adulthood. This disorder is manifested in at least five of the following ways:

- making frantic attempts to avoid actual or imagined abandonment by another person;
- repeatedly developing intense but unstable relationships with others in which the person vacillates between idealizing the other person and devaluing him or her;
- persisting with a very unstable self-image, to the point of having an identity disturbance;
- reacting very impulsively in a potentially self-damaging manner in more than one area of life;
- repeating self-mutilating behavior or suicidal gestures or threats;
- regularly displaying highly unstable and shifting mood states, such as intense displeasure, irritability, or anxiety;
- experiencing empty feelings repeatedly;
- having difficulty in controlling anger or displaying inappropriate strong anger, extreme sarcasm, enduring bitterness, or verbal outbursts—this anger is typically displayed when a lover is perceived as abandoning, withholding, neglecting, or being uncaring;
- temporary paranoid suspiciousness or dissociative symptoms under periods of stress.

Some of these individuals develop psychotic-like symptoms during especially stressful times. Some of these individuals derive more security from "transitional objects" such as a pet or inanimate object. The childhood backgrounds of adults with a Borderline Personality have greater frequencies of sexual abuse, neglect, physical abuse, early parental loss or separation, and hostile family conflict than the general population.

Clinical psychologist is a professional and a scientist who holds an earned doctoral degree (Ph.D., or Psy.D.) in psychology from an accredited university, with a one year clinical internship training and at least one year of post-doctoral training or supervised practice, in order to specialize in the study, diagnosis and treatment of mental, emotional, and behavioral disorders. Clinical psychologists are uniquely trained and experienced in administering and interpreting psychological tests to assess personality, intelligence, and neuropsychological functioning. They also render individual psychotherapy, group therapy, behavior therapy, marital therapy, hypnosis, biofeedback, and other psychological therapies. They are typically required to pass examinations for state licensure to practice their profession.

Common law is the "case law" which is declared to be law by the court system. It has its roots in the established legal tradition and customs in

England, and it was brought over to the English colonies and has carried forward to court practice today.

Competence is the legal recognition of a person's capacity to perform some specific task. Competence is not determined generally for a person, but is specifically determined for a certain type of demand. For example, one specific type of competence is the ability of a defendant to assist his or her attorney in preparing one's defense. Another kind of competence would be the capability to give informed consent for a medical or legal matter.

Conscious means alert, awake, and aware of external surroundings.

Consensual is a legal term indicating mutual voluntary, competent, and informed consent.

Consent must legally include 1) agreement based upon full disclosure of information, 2) voluntary agreement with no coercion, and 3) competence of the persons involved to make the agreement.

Crohn's disease is a painful inflammation of the intestinal tract; an inflammation of the ileum, a part of the bowel, or of the mucous and submucous tissues of the small intestines.

Delusion is a false belief that is firmly believed by an individual despite obvious proof or evidence to the contrary. It is a belief that is not ordinarily accepted by other people in one's culture.

Denial is an automatic psychological defense maneuver whereby the person consciously or unconsciously denies anxiety or conflict to protect oneself from the awareness of internal or external stressors.

Dependent personality disorder is a diagnosis listed in the *Diagnostic and Statistical Manual of Mental Disorders, Fourth Edition,* which refers to a pervasive and longstanding lack of self-confidence, with an excessive need to have other people assume responsibility for one's life. It includes a tendency to subordinate one's own needs and desires to the person(s) on whom one depends. An individual with this disorder displays clinging and submissive behavior, and harbors strong fears of separation from others. This behavior pattern is meant to draw caregiving from others and is motivated by a perception of oneself as someone who is unable to do well without a great deal of help from others. The pattern begins in early adulthood and is indicated by at least five of the following characteristics:

- When the person experiences the end of a close relationship, he or she urgently seeks out another person to depend upon for support and care.
- The person has unrealistic preoccupations with fears of being left alone to fend for himself or herself.

- The person feels very helpless or very uncomfortable when they are alone, due to unrealistic fears of being incompetent to care for himself or herself.
- The person will repeatedly go to great lengths to draw nurturing and emotional support from other people.
- The person has trouble starting things on his or her own, due to a profound lack of self-confidence in his abilities or in his judgments.
- The person finds it very difficult to disagree with other people because of a fear of losing approval or emotional support from others.
- The person struggles to make everyday decisions if they do not receive an excessive amount of reassurance, advice, and guidance from other people.
- The person experiences a strong need to have other people assume major responsibility for most areas of his or her life.

Depression refers to emotions of sadness, discouragement, and despair. Depression can occur as a normal reaction to circumstances, or can be a secondary syndrome to another disorder, or can be a symptom of a specific mental disorder. See *Major Depression*, and *Dysthymia*.

Determinism is the unproven assumption that all human behavior is caused ("determined") by the person's heredity and/or environment. Determinism is a practical operating assumption made by much behavioral and social scientific research studies, in order to conduct experiments. Radical determinism leaves no place for true human responsibility, which is assumed by the American legal system.

Dissociative disorder or dissociation is a clinical term which describes a disruption of the usually integrated functions of mental process whereby the person's mind prevents certain experiences or memories from entering conscious awareness because of the uncomfortable anxiety connected with that experience or with that memory.

Dysfunctional family is an abnormal, impaired, or incompletely functioning family unit, characterized by conflicts between family members, poor communication between members, violation of family boundaries (such as children behaving as parents or vice versa), and lack of appropriate emotional support between members.

Dysthymic disorder is a diagnosis listed in the *Diagnostic and Statistical Manual of Mental Disorders, Fourth Edition,* which refers to a long-standing depressed mood that occurs on the majority of days for at least two years. During the days the person experiences a depressed mood, he or she has at least two of these symptoms:

- low self-esteem

- difficulty making decisions or poor concentration
- overeating or poor appetite
- oversleeping or sleep disturbance
- fatigue or low energy
- feelings of hopelessness

The person's symptoms cause impaired functioning socially or on the job, or the person experiences significant distress.

Epilepsy is a recurring disorder of brain function that results in repeated, sudden, brief seizures. The seizure pattern may be attacks or altered consciousness, motor movements, or altered sensory experiences.

Expert witness is a person who is allowed to present opinions in a court case on matters of fact that are considered to be beyond the level of expert knowledge of the ordinary citizen.

Fatal battered child profile is one profile of parents who kill their child in which physical abuse causes so much injury that the child dies, whether or not the parent intended to kill the child.

Filicide is the crime of murdering one's own child.

Forensic means belonging to courts of law, or being associated with the courts.

Forensic pathologist is a physician who specializes in the relations between medicine and law, as in conducting autopsies, or in determining the cause of death or the time of death.

Forensic psychiatrist is a physician who specializes in the branch of psychiatry which deals with the evaluation of mental and emotional illness related to criminal and civil legal situations. They serve as expert witnesses in court proceedings providing expert opinions on issues such as competence to stand trial, psychiatric diagnosis at the time of a crime, determination of insanity, and degree of responsibility for criminal conduct.

Forensic psychologist is a professional and a scientist who typically holds an earned doctoral degree (Ph.D. or Psy.D.) in psychology from an accredited university, who specializes in the study and diagnosis of mental, emotional, and behavior disorders related to legal situations, both civil and criminal. Forensic psychologists are uniquely trained and experienced in administering and interpreting psychological tests to assess personality, intelligence, and neuropsychological functioning with respect to criminal conduct, competence, and responsibility versus insanity. They serve as expert witnesses in court proceedings. In most states they are required to pass examinations for state licensure to practice their profession.

Genetic loading refers to genes and to inherited characteristics or tendencies.

Grieving is a normal, appropriate emotional process to a recognized personal loss. It generally subsides gradually and lasts only a period of months, and is distinguished from *depression* or *major depression*.

Guilt can refer either to 1) the emotion that results from doing what one believes is wrong, which can be accompanied by the need for punishment or feelings of worthlessness, or 2) objective moral guilt as a result of the violation of a government's laws or religious commandments.

"Guilty but mentally ill" is a legal verdict in a criminal case in which the person's mental impairment contributes to a crime such that a person is unable to control one's acts. This verdict can result in the same punishments as a "guilty" verdict, but the individual would receive psychiatric treatment prior to serving the sentence for the crime. This verdict recognizes that mental illness may not be judged to excuse the individual from legal responsibility for a criminal act or domestic matter.

Hallucination is seeing, hearing, smelling, tasting, or feeling the touch of something that seems real, but occurs in the absence of any genuine external stimulus.

Hearsay is a legal court term referring to any spoken or written statement made by a person who is not under an official oath to tell the truth. Usually, these unsworn statements are not allowed into evidence in a trial because they are considered to be unreliable. However, a common exception to the exclusion of hearsay statements is that expert witnesses are permitted to rely on and repeat hearsay statements in order to formulate their expert opinion and their testimony.

Hypervigilance is being excessively and unrealistically watchful or "on guard."

Incest is sexual activity between close, but unmarried, family relatives, such as father-daughter, mother-son, or between brother and sister.

Infanticide is the crime of murder of one's own baby.

Insanity is a legal concept and not a diagnostic term of psychiatry or clinical psychology. In simplest terms, a person is judged to be insane at the time of a crime if at the time he or she could not recognize right from wrong and would perform the crime even if a police officer were present. If a criminal defendant is judged to be insane, he or she is excused from the misconduct on the basis of his or her impaired mental condition at the time of the crime. The most widely used insanity defense standards in the United States are 1) the American Law Institute test, and 2) the M'Naghten tests. The American Law Institute formulation states that a person is not held responsible for a crime if a mental disease or defect at the time makes him unable to appreciate the wrongfulness of his act or deprives him of the capacity to conform his conduct to the requirements of the law. The M'Naghten tests or rules were historically introduced in the British House of Lords in 1843 to clarify the conditions under which a defense on the grounds of insanity must be proved; a person is not held responsible for a crime if he or she acted with a mental defect as not to know what he or she was doing, or if able to know the act, he or she did not know that it was wrong. In the state of South Carolina, if a person accused of a crime is found to have a mental disease or defect which renders him or her unable to distinguish moral or legal right from moral or legal wrong, or if that mental disease or defect renders him or her unable to recognize the particular act charged as morally or legally wrong, that person would be found "not guilty by reason of insanity."

Insanity defense is the argument of a criminal defendant to be excused for his misconduct on the basis of his mental condition.

Intermittent depression is a depressed mood state, which stops and starts again at intervals, such that the individual fluctuates between normal and depressed mood states repeatedly over time.

Interrogation is the interviewing of a criminal suspect by law enforcement officers.

Involuntary manslaughter is a lesser crime than murder, in which an individual unintentionally kills another person out of recklessness rather than from malice.

Irrational means lacking reason or contrary to reason; absurd; senseless.

"Lewd act on a minor" is a crime of performing an indecent, illegal sexual behavior with a child who has not reached the age of legal adulthood; see *sexual abuse.*

Major depression is a diagnosis listed in the *Diagnostic and Statistical Manual of Mental Disorders, Fourth Edition,* which refers to a condition for two weeks or more of having a depressed mood (feeling sad, empty, tearful, or irritable) or a great loss of interest in normal activities, plus at least four of the following symptoms:

- a significant change in body weight or a significant loss of normal appetite;
- a disturbed sleeping pattern or oversleeping;

- observable restlessness or a significant slowing down of activity;

- fatigue or loss of energy;

- feelings of worthlessness or inappropriate guilt;

- difficulty in thinking, concentrating, or decision-making;

- recurring thoughts about death, or suicidal thoughts and/or suicidal attempt.

The symptom pattern must occur nearly daily in the absence of any medical condition or drugs that could be a cause of the mood state. The depression must be at a level that causes significant distress or impairment in functioning in normal everyday life situations. While normal grieving can result in many of these same symptoms, it is not considered a major depression unless it lasts more than two months.

Malingering is a deliberate faking or exaggeration of an illness for the selfish purpose of obtaining some kind of personal gain or to avoid an unpleasant or undesired situation.

Manic-depressive illness is the older term for what is now known as "bipolar disorder."

Manipulative is an adjective referring to behaving in a shrewd or cunning manner, especially in a fraudulent or unfair way, for one's own selfish purposes or benefit.

Mens rea is a legal term referring to the ability of a person to form the intention to act. A person is held legally responsible for his or her own behavior, if at the time of an act, that person had neither *actus reus* nor *mens rea* impaired. An individual's misconduct can be judged to be a crime only if he or she voluntarily performs a criminal act (*actus reus*) and has a guilty mind (*mens rea*) at the time of that act.

Mental disorder is a clinically significant behavioral or psychological pattern that occurs in a person that is accompanied by distress or impairs some important area of everyday functioning. The cause can be a psychological, genetic, physical, chemical, or biological abnormality. In the United States, the most commonly used classification system of mental disorders used by psychiatrists, psychologists, physicians, and psychiatric social workers is the *Diagnostic and Statistical Manual of Mental Disorders, Fourth Edition*, published by the American Psychiatric Association in 1994.

Mental illness is a commonly used synonym *for mental disorder*, usually used by health professionals or the general public.

Mental retardation is the condition of having a significantly below average level of intellectual functioning, which results in being less adaptive and less able to learn more complex skills and knowledge.

Mercy killing profile is one profile of parents who kill their children in which the parent reports that his or her motive was to relieve the child from some form of incurable physical suffering caused by a medical condition of the child.

Molestation is a nontechnical term for forms of *sexual abuse* other than sexual intercourse.

Multiple personality is a term for a rare kind of dissociative disorder in which the person takes on two or more distinct personalities at different times.

Murder is the unlawful killing of any person with malice of forethought. Malice is the intentional performance of an unlawful act with intent of harm, and suggests hatred, wickedness, or intent to do wrong. Malice can be inferred if a person takes the life of an innocent person.

Nonlethal suicidal gesture is the term for a self-injurious action that the person says was meant to kill himself or herself, but that had little or no possibility of actually causing death. An example would be swallowing a number of pills or a type of pill that cannot cause death.

Nonverbal behavior is an unspoken action that can communicate feelings, attitudes, or meaning to another person in the same culture.

"Not guilty by reason of insanity" (often abbreviated as NGRI) is a legal verdict in a criminal case in which the defendant is judged to be insane at the time of a crime because at the time he or she could not recognize right from wrong. The person accused of a crime is thereby excused for the misconduct on the basis of his or her impaired mental condition at the time of the crime. In the state of South Carolina, if a criminal defendant is found to have a mental disease or defect which deprives him or her of the ability to distinguish moral or legal right from moral or legal wrong, or if that mental disease or defect renders him or her unable to recognize the particular act charged as morally or legally wrong, that person can be judged to be "not guilty by reason of insanity." (see **Insanity**)

Obsession is an unwanted but persisting idea or impulse that the person cannot stop by logical reasoning.

Oxymoron is a figure of speech in which contradictory ideas are combined, such as "sweet sorrow," or "thunderous silence," or "murdering mother."

Panic is a sudden, intense fearfulness, terror, or anxiety, which is so overwhelming that it creates a feeling of terror with psychological changes such as shortness of breath, smothering sensations, pounding heart, accelerated heart rate, chest discomfort, or choking. The person can feel that he or she is "going crazy" or losing control.

Paranoia is a rare mental condition in which a person gradually develops a complicated system of thinking based on *mis*interpretation of a real event. This is a long-standing condition that does not seem to interfere with most other thinking and personality.

Perpetrator is a term that refers to the person who performs a crime, or who is guilty of committing a hoax.

Persecutory delusion is a *delusion* (see above definition) or misperception that oneself (or someone closely associated with the person) is the object of being attacked, cheated, persecuted, harassed, or conspired against.

Personality is the long-term characteristic way that a person thinks, feels, and behaves. It is a rather ingrained and repeated pattern of behavior or way of adapting to one's world.

Plea bargain is a term for the process and for the result of agreeing to enter a specific guilty plea to a crime in exchange for a specified agreed-upon sentence. For example, Susan V. Smith's defense lawyer, David Bruck, attempted to obtain a plea bargain agreement from the prosecutor, Tommy Pope, in which Susan would plead guilty to double murder in exchange for a life sentence with possibility of parole. Mr. Pope rejected the offer, so no plea bargain was achieved for this case.

Postconcussion syndrome or **postconcussional disorder** is a medical condition that is present after a traumatic injury to the brain from impact with an object, in which the individual may suffer temporary or prolonged loss of consciousness or other loss of brain function. Neuropsychological testing typically confirms difficulty in concentration, shifting focus of attention, or memory difficulties. For the first three months following the trauma, the person suffers three or more of the following:

- disordered sleep
- headache
- becoming easily fatigued
- dizziness or sensations of vertigo
- irritability or aggressiveness with little or no provocation
- apathy or lack of spontaneity
- mood states of depression, anxiety, or rapid mood changes
- changes in personality, such as sexual inappropriateness

The condition causes significant impairment in functioning.

Premenstrual dysphoric disorder is a research diagnostic category in which a variety of dysfunctional mood states, including depression, are repeatedly found in correlation with certain points in a woman's menstrual cycle.

Prevalence has to do with the frequency of a disorder, and refers to the total number of cases of a certain disorder for a specific population at a given time.

Promiscuity refers to the characteristic of engaging in sexual relations with many individuals.

Prozac is a medication prescribed for treating depression.

Psychiatrist is a licensed physician who has received several years of postgraduate training in psychiatry beyond the M.D. or D.O. degree in order to specialize in the diagnosis and treatment of mental and emotional disorders.

Psychiatric evaluation is an interview procedure conducted by a psychiatrist for the purpose of assessing for a mental disorder or to answer a specific consultation question or court order regarding an individual.

Psychiatric hospitalization is the treatment of a mental disorder on an inpatient basis in a hospital or hospital unit staffed with professionals from the several fields such as medicine, psychiatry, clinical psychology, psychiatric nursing, occupational therapy, art therapy, music therapy, and psychiatric social work.

Psychogenic fugue is a long-term amnesia state caused by psychological facts in which the person leaves his or her home, changes their lifestyle and conduct, with almost total loss of memory regarding their former life, although skills are retained. Once the fugue state ends, the person completely recalls their pre-fugue memory and forgets the whole fugue period of time.

Psychological assessment, or psychological evaluation is conducted by a psychologist and involves the diagnostic procedures of clinical interviews, review of clinical records, and the administration and interpretation of psychological tests. The evaluation is targeted to answer a specific set of referral questions by a physician, the court, or a probation officer, for example.

Psychologist is a professional and scientist who typically holds an earned doctoral degree (Ph.D., or Psy.D.) in psychology from an accredited university, who specializes in the study, diagnosis and treatment of thoughts, emotions, and behaviors. There are many subspecialties within the broad discipline of psychology, including clinical psychology, counseling psychology, forensic psychology, school psychology, educational psychology, industrial psychology, developmental psychology, social psychology, physiological psychology, experimental psychology, and health psychology. Clinical psychologists and forensic psychologists are uniquely trained and experienced in administering and interpreting psychological tests to assess personality, intelligence, and neuropsychological functioning. In most states psychologists are required to pass examinations for state licensure before they are allowed to practice their profession.

Psychotic parent profile is one profile of parents who kill their child in which a psychotic condition (such as postpartum psychosis or postpartum depression with psychotic features) renders the parent out of contact with reality at the time of the killing of the child.

Psychosis is a broad inclusive term for a category of major mental disorders in which a person experiences significant impairment in his or her ability to think, interpret reality, remember, communicate, respond emotionally, and behave appropriately, such that the person is unable to meet ordinary life demands. The cause can be biological or psychological. The person suffering a psychosis can have delusions, hallucinations, impulse control difficulty, and inappropriate mood states.

Repentance is a theological term which involves a change of mind, affections, convictions and commitment in a person to the extent of turning away from a past wrong course of action or living to turn toward a relationship with God.

Repression is an automatic psychological defense maneuver operating unconsciously that banishes unacceptable ideas or impulses from consciousness. This psychological process protects oneself from awareness of internal or external stresses.

Retaliating/manipulating parent profile is one profile of parents who kill their child with the motive of wanting to cause the child's father permanent suffering, or the motive to pose as a victim to obtain their illicit lover's affection and thereby advance their romantic love life.

SLED stands for State Law Enforcement Division, which is the state-level organization of law enforcement in the state of South Carolina.

Stressor is a term for a distressing event (such as the end of a romantic relationship), or a cluster of distressing situations (such as serious marital conflicts or business difficulties). Some stressors are continuous, some are one-time events, and some recur over and over.

Suicidal attempt is a self-inflicted injury intended to take one's own life.

Suicidal gesture is a self-inflicted injury intended to look like a suicidal attempt but is actually a plea for help or a dramatic way to draw attention to oneself, without the actual intention to take one's own life. Some suicidal gestures can accidentally result in the individual's unintended death, as some speculate was the case with Harry Vaughan, Susan Vaughan Smith's biological father.

"Suicide by proxy" profile is one profile of parents who kill their child, in which the parent becomes so enmeshed with their child that they blur the boundaries between their own identity and the child's identity. When such a parent becomes severely depressed and suffers suicidal urges, they kill the child as a confused way of "killing a part of themselves."

Suppression is an automatic psychological defense maneuver of consciously putting an unacceptable impulse, thought or feeling out of one's mind to protect oneself from awareness of internal or external stressors.

Trial is a legal proceeding that takes place in a government courtroom to determine the facts and legal questions related to a criminal indictment or civil complaint.

Unconscious is the part of the mind that is subject to no awareness or only rare awareness by the individual. This represents the thoughts and memories that have never been conscious or that have been conscious but have been subsequently repressed. See *repression*.

Victim is a person who is injured or otherwise harmed by, or suffers from, some circumstance or some act perpetrated by another individual(s).

"Victim mentality" is a lay term used by the public to describe the thinking pattern of a person who takes the "victim stance." The "victim mentality" is the line of thinking taken in an attempt to remove responsibility from common criminals.

"Victim stance" is a lay term used by the public to refer to posturing as a victim in order to obtain the social benefits people normally give to victims. The "victim stance" is usually a matter of pretending to be a victim when one is not really a victim. In other circumstances, a genuine victim can take a "victim stance" by drawing attention to one's victimization for the potential benefits that may come along with other people recognizing one as a victim. Or, a person may take a "victim stance" by exaggerating the effects of being a victim, or trying to be excused for one's irresponsible or illegal behavior inappropriately by drawing attention to one's past victimization, as is done with the "abuse excuse."

About the Author

George Rekers, Ph.D., is a tenured professor of neuropsychiatry and behavioral science at the University of South Carolina, School of Medicine and a clinical psychologist in the teaching hospital—the Hall Psychiatric Institute—which provided the court-ordered mental health evaluation for Susan Smith, which was entered into evidence during her trial. Because of a court "gag" order prohibiting the doctors who personally evaluated Smith from releasing their findings, and in light of his clinical expertise and experience as an expert witness in court cases, Dr. Rekers was designated, through the university media relations office, to be the spokesperson to the press regarding the mental evaluation procedures.

Dr. Rekers is a Fellow of the Academy of Clinical Psychology, with twenty-three years of clinical experience in conducting psychological evaluations and in rendering psychotherapy. He is well qualified and experienced in communicating to the lay public. He has translated complex psychological knowledge to patients in lay language and is the author of seven published books for the lay public. Dr. Rekers's most recent book is an academic volume, *Handbook on Child and Adolescent Sexual Problems*, published by Lexington Books/Simon and Schuster in April 1995.

Professor Rekers received his Ph.D. in psychology from UCLA in 1972, and was honored to be a Visiting Scholar in clinical psychology at Harvard University. He was previously an associate professor and chief psychologist at the University of Florida College of Medicine. He has delivered invited expert testimony before committees of the U.S. House of Representatives and the U.S. Senate, and has served as an invited advisor to the White House Domestic Policy Council, the Attorney General's Task Force, and various cabinet agencies. Professor Rekers has been awarded major research grants from the National Institute of Mental Health, and he has been an invited lecturer at universities, research institutes, and academies in Europe, Africa, and Asia, including Austria, Czechoslovakia, the former Soviet Republic of Estonia, the Netherlands, Poland, Russia, the Republic of Slovakia, the Republic of South Africa, Spain, the Royal Kingdom of Swaziland, the former Soviet Academy of Sciences, and the World Laboratory.

One area of Professor Rekers's expertise is the emotional effects of child sexual abuse upon individuals in their adulthood—a central issue in the Smith defense case.